A NEW
PROTESTANT
LABOR
ETHIC AT
WORK

A NEW PROTESTANT LABOR ETHIC AT WORK

Ken Estey

THE
PILGRIM
PRESS
Cleveland

The Pilgrim Press
700 Prospect Avenue East
Cleveland, Ohio 44115-1100
pilgrimpress.com

Printed in the United States of America on acid-free paper

07   06   05   04   03   02   5   4   3   2   1

Library of Congress Cataloging-in-Publication Data

Estey, Ken, 1961-
    A new protestant labor ethic at work / Ken Estey.
      p. cm.
    Includes bibliographical references and index.
    ISBN 0-8298-1439-6 (pbk. : alk. paper)
    1. Work ethic. 2. Capitalism – Religious aspects – Protestant churches.
3. Quality of work life. 4. Protestant work ethic. 5. Industrial relations – United
States. 6. Working class – United States. 7. Dignity.   I. Title.

  HD4905 .E85 2002
  306.3'613 – dc21

                            2002029072

CONTENTS

PREFACE

The goal of this book is to propose a labor ethic that places the accent on the "protest" in Protestantism. This ethic intends to interrupt the forced march of the Protestant work ethic, the dominant cultural ideal in the United States. Protestantism must not be about capitulation to capitalism. It must engage in activities of protest or challenge to the economic powers in our time. A new "Protestant labor ethic at work" needs to question and confront authority so as to help undo and delegitimate the newest (and oldest) forms of dehumanization as it pertains to workers and workplace conditions. A specific focus in this book will be on an emerging consensus in Christian business ethics: covenantal ethics. Using the Saturn Corporation as an important case study and other historical resources, this book will argue that a covenantal business ethic is an insufficient resource for workers. It needs to be replaced by an ethic that upholds explicitly the positive possibilities of emphasizing workers' interests and workplace resistance.

The study of ethics becomes most compelling when it addresses the basic concerns of people who struggle, day by day, to live their lives with dignity. The workplace is the primary arena for the intense conflict over issues such as safety, respect, and a wage that lifts life well above drudgery and daily despair. Millions of people work full-time but still do not earn enough to avoid poverty and the grim prospects beckoned by a minimum wage. People die at work, and they die because of work. Many do not have work and would endure much hardship to gain or keep a position on the rickety wage ladder.

Beverly Harrison, my advisor and teacher at Union Theological Seminary, has been an inspiration for this project. Her early encouragement to consider carefully the distinction between "work" as a theological category and "labor" as a historical-material activity has been most influential. Rather than urging me to rely solely on my theological training to ponder the problem of work, she has helped me to value my life experience as a source for the transformation of the conditions of labor. Instead of increasing my alienation from the working class, her influence has caused me to embrace the practical activity of identifying with my working-class background. Michael Zweig of the Department of Economics at the State University of New York, Stony Brook, and founding member of the Group for the Study of Working Class Life also helped me to recognize this life advantage. This alone opened up avenues of exploration that I had not considered previously. Donald Shriver of Union Theological Seminary shares my interest in labor issues, and he alerted me to others who are working in the field. Larry Rasmussen, also of Union, has emphasized the historical, lived aspect of ethics.

M. B. Walsh and Matthew Ally read the earliest drafts of this book. M. B.'s suggestions and critiques were insightful, and she helped me to define ways to keep the project on track. Matthew's enormous patience enabled him to endure successive drafts. This will always be appreciated as well as the many discussions that we have had on the relationship between ethics and history. Tom Reiber's enthusiasm for my project renewed my energy at many points. He helped me to see the potential for this book and his encouragement not to be reticent has been a liberating influence. Gabriella Lettini and Annie Rawlings offered sound advice that helped me clarify the direction of the first part of the book. Gabriella has helped me be mindful of the international perspective, particularly the *millions* of Italian workers who filled the streets in protest in the spring of 2002. Annie's work at the Bertram M. Beck Institute on Religion and Poverty in New York City is a rich resource for anyone concerned about religion, poverty, work, and welfare. Jeff Ross, a lifelong friend, an automobile aficionado, a caring comrade — to him, many thanks for his steady support and faithful presence. Bourque deserves mention for his oft-stated point that this pursuit was not for the birds and Kolya for his emphasis that "roses are great, but I want bread too."

I also thank the workers of United Auto Workers (UAW) Local 1853 of the Saturn Corporation who risked their jobs to talk honestly about working conditions at Saturn. Their contributions have been central to the development of this book. I think particularly of Sheryle, who opened the door to my understanding of the real Saturn and its work ethic.

Drew Kadel (formerly of Union) and Seth Kasten, head of reader services and reference and research librarian of the Burke Library at Union Theological Seminary, provided unmatched reference help on many occasions. Timothy Staveteig of The Pilgrim Press expressed an interest in this work at a very early stage, which provided the encouragement that I needed to persist. George R. Graham, the editor, steadily guided this project to completion. He taught me more than I thought there was to know about book production. For his dedication and for enduring with me all the twists and turns of fate that accompanied the writing of this book, I extend to him my heartfelt gratitude. I thank John Eagleson for his expertise and his patience at the final stages of this project.

I thank the staff and owners, Panagiotis and Wendy Binioris, of the Hungarian Pastry Shop. Located across the street from the Cathedral Church of St. John the Divine in New York City, "the Hungarian" is an oasis for writers, conversationalists, and intellectuals. They have been unfailingly hospitable with endless cups of coffee and the space to ponder alone, and with friends and colleagues. While a writer writes alone, almost all books emerge from within a community.

Finally, I thank Lorena E. Cuevas for everything that she did to make it possible to complete this project. Without her contributions, this book would still be in progress. She is my dear wife and ally in the global struggle. As a Chilena, she knows that there is another September 11. In 1973, over three thousand Chileans were killed and tortured with the help of the United States in the coup that crushed working-class struggles and toppled democratically elected president Salvador Allende. To quote from graffiti that we observed on a municipal building in Santiago: *En homenaje a los caídos se levantan nuevos combatientes.*

I dedicate this book to her.

GOOD NEWS
FOR A WORKING WORLD?

===

What price do the industrial workers pay for our prosperity?
— Harry Ward (1918)[1]

This book is for Protestant workers and all workers in the United States, of whatever religious persuasion, who have been crushed under the work ethic. The labor ethic proposed in this book is part of a general "protestant project" that highlights the positive possibilities of worker resistance and struggle against any circumstance, person, or institution that alienates individuals from themselves or separates people from each other in the workplace. If workers can come to a clearer understanding of the ways to engage in projects of emancipation and freedom-making in the workplace, then a work ethic, Protestant or otherwise, could be said to work. Such tasks will not be easy. New bonds arise with the breaking of old ones. The most virulent forms of authority are remarkable for their iron grip.

It is important to speak as plainly as possible about such matters. A "Protestant labor ethic at work" opposes a Protestant work ethic that values hard work but devalues workers and leaves them with no recourse when denied safe conditions, living wages, or self-determination in the workplace. This book is an examination of the problems with an emerging trend in Protestant reflection on work — covenantal business ethics. This ethic suggests that workplace relationships ought to take their inspiration from a theologically and biblically informed emphasis on mutuality, cooperation, common interests, and the sharing of power

---

1. The title of this chapter is based on Harry Frederick Ward's *The Gospel for a Working World* (New York: Missionary Education Movement of the United States and Canada, 1918). This quote is from p. 6.

1

between labor and management. On the surface, such a position seems fair. But a closer look at the working world reveals a pattern of sanctioned exploitation. The interests of owners and managers trumps that of workers.

My years in a white working-class family in rural New Hampshire continue to challenge and provoke me as I consider the church and its relationship to work and the labor movement. In my conservative evangelical Protestant church, we were taught that "correct" theological beliefs and a "good work ethic" were the cornerstones of an eternally true morality that would make stability and happiness possible. My parents called the social and cultural shifts in American life in the 1960s the "new morality." For them, this was another name for the "old immorality." They did not understand or respond to the profound economic realignments also occurring at this time. The teaching and practice of my church community had nothing to do with the work experiences of my parents' generation.

Sermons or Bible studies rarely featured the issue of one's work. There were no public avenues to discuss problems at work or to organize for solutions. Whether one's work was somewhat satisfying or simply unbearable, church served only as a temporary haven removed from the stresses and strains of work life, which people were expected to weather alone. Karen L. Bloomquist addresses this situation with clarity and insight: "Although religious yearnings arise out of one's plight in the world, religion is usually viewed as compartmentalized from one's life in the world. It offers the promise of an eventual escape. Getting to heaven, where one receives one's compensation, becomes the means of escape from domination."[2] Such a view of religion makes it very difficult to see that socially constructed personal deprivation is, indeed, a public matter.

Many workers in the United States also believe that difficulties in the workplace are only private matters. The widely used phrases "private enterprise" and the "private sector" are accomplices to the idea that workplace matters are not aspects of the "public realm." Rather they can be handled "internally" by one's immediate supervisor or the company's human resource department. The problems created by regarding the workplace and its issues as private are immense and far-reaching. One

---

2. Karen L. Bloomquist, *The Dream Betrayed: Religious Challenge of the Working Class* (Minneapolis: Fortress Press, 1990), 42.

of the many reasons for this state of affairs includes the dramatic decline in the number of unionized laborers in the United States. In turn, this leads to a diminishing sense of solidarity with other workers. The sense of a common plight among workers has eroded steadily over the past three decades. The idea that an injury to one is an injury to all is neglected if not forgotten.[3] Workers are increasingly left to fend for themselves in a harsh "global village" that is deeply alienating and fraught with uncertainty.

My family did not belong to the labor movement. Solidarity was not based on the "brotherhood" of workers but on the belief that all were "brothers and sisters in Christ." Their adherence to a conservative theological agenda that focused on the need for individual salvation and personal sanctification only intensified the problems that they experienced. The few resources in evangelicalism in the United States that do reflect on the workplace turn time and again to issues of obedience to authority and the responsibility of the *individual* Christian. Doug Sherman and William Hendricks's book *Your Work Matters to God* is one example: "We've already seen that as a Christ-follower, you work for Jesus; He is your Boss. . . . In practical terms, this means abiding by the rules and policies of your company, and carrying out the orders of those above you. It also includes obeying the law. . . . No matter how despicable those over us may behave, we must see that standing behind them is Christ Himself."[4]

Evangelical Protestant reflection on work neglects a critical appraisal of those who own and organize the structure of the workplace. Instead, it tends to focus on those who must endure the decisions made by others. Carl Henry, in *Aspects of Christian Social Ethics,* argued that the problem is not "technological displacement" but one of "spiritual estrangement." "The joylessness, the depressing drudgery of monotonous toil, are caused more by the worker than by the character of his work. 'Demechanization' is too simple a solution for the unbeliever's problem; valid 'personalizing' of work will come only with his own spiritual awakening."[5] Erwin Lutzer in *Coming to Grips with Your Role in the Workplace* echoes Henry's

---

3. See Kim Moody, *An Injury to All: The Decline of American Unionism* (London and New York: Verso, 1988).

4. Doug Sherman and William Hendricks, *Your Work Matters to God* (Colorado Springs: NavPress, 1990), 126.

5. Carl F. H. Henry, *Aspects of Christian Social Ethics* (Grand Rapids, Mich.: William B. Eerdmans, 1964), 60. Henry's book is one example of a conservative-evangelical view of work. Though written in the 1960s, it remains influential. Chuck Colson and Jack Eckerd

view: "If being a Christian cannot transform our attitude toward a job we dislike, then the promises of the New Testament are largely empty and Christ's credibility is tarnished.... If we yield ourselves to God and see our work from His perspective, we can have our attitude changed so that we can find fulfillment even in a job we don't enjoy."[6] The emphasis on obedience and the role of the individual worker leaves little room for organized resistance to systematic exploitation and mistreatment. Stanley Baldwin in *Take This Job and Love It* makes this very clear: "Reducing the volume or quality of work, however, smacks of vengeance, which the Bible forbids (see Rom 12:19). And dragging your feet on the job also violates the basic biblical principle for work.... 'Whatever you do, work at it with all your heart, as working for the Lord, not for men' (Col 3:23)."[7]

One would hope that a more balanced approach might be found in the "theologies of work" that have appeared periodically since the 1950s and particularly Marie-Dominique Chenu's classic *The Theology of Work: An Exploration* (1966).[8] These theologies try to connect human labor with the traditional doctrines of creation, justification, and sanctification.[9] They also highlight the ethical role of work with respect to self-identity, fulfillment, and personal meaning. The development of theologies of work would seem to be a useful first step in calling attention, within theological discourse, to the plight of laborers. Yet the inability to consider seriously empirical data on labor and laborers limits them. The voices and experiences of workers are ignored in favor of theological categories that describe idealized visions of work. The social and historical realities that shape the daily lives of workers are neglected. Most theologies of work assume that theological discussions of work can occur without sustained attention to the power dynamics that deeply affect workers and the structure of the workday. Theological or ethical

---

in *Why America Doesn't Work* (Dallas: Word Publishing, 1991) and Doug Sherman and William Hendricks (above) both cite him.

6. Erwin W. Lutzer, *Coming to Grips with Your Role in the Workplace* (Chicago: Moody Press, 1992), 30–31.

7. Stanley C. Baldwin, *Take This Job and Love It: Solving the Problems You Face at Work* (Downers Grove, Ill.: InterVarsity Press, 1988), 74.

8. Marie-Dominique Chenu, *The Theology of Work: An Exploration*, trans. Lilian Soirow (Chicago: H. Regnery, 1966).

9. Dorothee Soelle with Shirley A. Cloyes, *To Work and to Love: A Theology of Creation* (Philadelphia: Fortress Press, 1984). Also see Miroslav Volf, *Work in the Spirit: Toward a Theology of Work* (New York: Oxford University Press, 1991).

reflection alone cannot cause lasting alterations to the power dynamics that govern the work world.

There are some hopeful exceptions among those who propose a theology of work. One example includes Buti Tlhagale's essay, "Towards a Black Theology of Labour," in which he emphasizes worker resistance to the circumstances of their work. Instead of highlighting abstractly the co-creative dimension in the process of work, Tlhagale urges that workers should be co-creators in overturning the conditions of work that objectify them. He argues that workers must demand recognition agreements, participate in industrial councils, stage strikes, organize legitimate unions, reject company unions, and demand better wages. All of this creative activity, according to Tlhagale, is modeled on the liberator-God who acts in history.[10] As for the equation of labor and human dignity, any simple Christian claim about dignity in work is insufficient. "Self-assertive acts" — acts of workplace rebellion and resistance — all affirm the dignity of workers.[11]

Forays into other sources in the United States to find theological tools to critique the workplace have proved disappointing. For instance, the survey of covenantal business ethics in this book reveals more continuity with modern fundamentalist and evangelical reflection on work than most of its adherents would care to admit. The Christian ideals of love and cooperation dampen the ardor of many to challenge directly the extraordinary power of capital. Both liberals and conservatives share a persistent inability or unwillingness to challenge current economic practices in the United States. This state of affairs is alarming.

The issue of alienating work must be part of any labor ethic if it hopes to address the material conditions of people's daily lives. This book wishes to call attention to the new ways that work is patterned and organized so as to update descriptions of worker alienation. The

---

10. Buti Tlhagale, "Towards a Black Theology of Labour," in *The Three-Fold Cord: Theology, Work and Labour*, ed. James R. Cochrane and Gerald O. West (Hilton, South Africa: Cluster Publications, 1991), 144, 151.

11. Ibid., 152. Also see Barbara Hilkert Andolsen, *Good Work at the Video Display Terminal: A Feminist Ethical Analysis of Changes in Clerical Work* (Knoxville: University of Tennessee Press, 1989). See her essay "Feminist Theological Reflections on Justice and Solidarity with Women Workers" in *Organization Man, Organization Woman: Calling, Leadership, and Culture* (Nashville: Abingdon Press, 1997), 81–96. Also Barbara Paleczny, *Clothed in Integrity: Weaving Just Cultural Relations and the Garment Industry* (Waterloo, Ontario: Wilfrid Laurier University Press, 2000), Bloomquist, *The Dream Betrayed*, and John C. Raines and Donna C. Day-Lower, *Modern Work and Human Meaning* (Philadelphia: Westminster Press, 1986).

focus will be on workplace relationships in companies that emphasize employee involvement in areas once solely the province of management. The ways that laborers become estranged from each other and ignore their collective interests will be considered. This book will also explore a key contradiction: efforts to achieve harmonious relations in the workplace may dissolve relationships in an atmosphere of mistrust and fear. A Christian ethic which, in the spirit of love, promotes cooperation and harmonious work relationships without accounting for the unequal distribution of power and privilege between workers and managers (and owners of capital) will inevitably side with the interests and goals of capital. This is a characteristic problem of covenantal ethics, and it must be challenged. Such an ethic offers little possibility for ameliorating or changing the material conditions that fragment workers. The viewpoint that cooperation as a norm and a practice for workers should be privileged over conflict and adversarial relationships between workers and owners (or managers) of capital is troublesome at best. Given the current development of capitalism in the United States, cooperation is not an adequate Christian ethical norm to guide the relationship between labor and capital in the modern U.S. workplace. How insightful can Protestant Christian ethics be in discerning ways to improve the lot of workers if they presuppose that capital and labor have shared interests when, in fact, their interests are in constant conflict?

The Protestant Ethic

A "Protestant labor ethic at work" depends upon an understanding of the Protestant ethic, but it is not about resurrecting what Max Weber described in his classic *The Protestant Ethic and The Spirit of Capitalism* (1904–5). The "Protestant ethic" is a term that describes a larger project to show how "ideas become effective forces in society."[12] This approach is meant to avoid the economistic tendencies in certain types of Marxism that explained historical circumstances solely in terms of economic laws. He also wanted to challenge the specious arguments that the Reformation, by itself, led directly to capitalism.

Weber wished to explore how "religious forces have taken part in the qualitative formation and the quantitative expansion of that spirit over

---

12. Max Weber, *The Protestant Ethic and the Spirit of Capitalism*, trans. Talcott Parsons (New York: Charles Scribner's Sons, 1958), 90–91.

the world."[13] The Protestant ethic is a religious force, and it encompasses notions such as vocation, work, predestination, salvation, and asceticism. "But God requires social achievement of the Christian because He wills that social life shall be organized according to His commandments, in accordance with that purpose. The social activity of the Christian in the world is solely activity *in majorem gloriam Dei.* This character is hence shared by labour in a calling which serves the mundane life of the community."[14] For Weber, the practice of thrift, industriousness, self-control, temperance, and fortitude are also part of the Protestant ethic. For its adherents, such practices enable a partnership with God in the unfolding of God's plan for the world. This partnership includes one's life work in a vocation or calling to serve others.

To understand the historical connection between the Protestant ethic and "everyday economic conduct," Weber looked to Richard Baxter (1615–91).[15] He exemplified, for Weber, the Puritan idea of calling and the ascetic way of life that this calling entailed. Weber took particular note of his injunctions to glorify God and to engage in hard and continuous bodily or mental labor. Socializing, idle talk, luxury, and sleeping more than six to eight hours are all to be avoided. A Presbyterian minister, he is known for refusing a bishopric under the English Restoration and for his lengthy tomes on Christianity and morality. *A Christian Directory* and particularly *The Saints' Everlasting Rest* spell out plainly the duty of Christians. Everlasting rest is only for the next life. To rest in this world or to be self-satisfied amid the accumulation of one's wealth is odious because it is only in the presence of God that all desires can be met.[16] In *A Christian Directory,* the poor are directed to be "laborious and diligent" in their callings and to cheerfully serve God even in the "meanest work." The rich are instructed not to live in unprofitable idleness but to "labour as constantly as the poor."[17] In *The Saints' Everlasting Rest,* Baxter notes that "if you were but busied in your lawful callings you would not be so ready to hearken to temptations; much less if you were busied above with God. Will you leave your plough and harvest in the field, or leave the quenching of a fire in your houses, to run with

---

13. Ibid., 91.
14. Ibid., 108.
15. Ibid., 155.
16. Ibid., 260, n. 8.
17. Richard Baxter, *Chapters from A Christian Directory or A Summ of Practical Theology and Cases of Conscience,* ed. Jeannette Tawney (London: G. Bell, 1925), 47, 54.

children a hunting of butterflies? Would a judge be persuaded to rise from the bench, when he is sitting upon life and death, to go and play among the boys in the streets? . . . Employment is one of the saints' chief preservatives against temptation."[18]

For Baxter, the issue of one's work was of prime theological importance. The most eloquent and oft-quoted passages of Weber's classic book refer to the disconnection between work and theology. He speaks almost wistfully of the people of Baxter's time: "The Puritan wanted to work in a calling; we are forced to do so." And, "In Baxter's view the care for external goods should only lie on the shoulders of the 'saint like a light cloak, which can be thrown aside at any moment.' But fate decreed that the cloak should become an iron cage."[19] Ernst Troeltsch, a contemporary and friend of Max Weber, offers this perspective in *The Social Teaching of the Christian Churches*:

> From the economic and social point of view the consequences of this conception of the "calling" were extraordinary. It raised the ordinary work of one's profession (within one's vocation) and the ardour with which secular work was prosecuted to the level of a religious duty in itself; from a mere method of providing for material needs it became an end in itself, providing scope for the exercise of faith within the labour of the "calling." That gave rise to that ideal of work for work's sake which forms the intellectual and moral assumption which lies behind the modern bourgeois way of life.[20]

Troeltsch's notion of "work for work's sake" goes to the heart of our current terminology of "work ethic." Weber rightly viewed modern labor as a forced ethic. He noted that "[The modern economic] order is now bound to the technical and economic conditions of machine production

---

18. Richard Baxter, *The Saints' Everlasting Rest* (1650), abridged with an Introduction by John T. Wilkinson (London: Epworth Press, 1962), 112. For a mordant rebuttal to the work ethic, see Paul Lafargue (Karl Marx's Cuban-born son-in-law), *The Right to Be Lazy* (Chicago: Charles H. Kerr, 1907). For insight on the work ethic as experienced by enslaved women, see Joan M. Martin, *More Than Chains and Toil: A Christian Work Ethic of Enslaved Women* (Louisville: Westminster John Knox Press, 2000).

19. Weber, *The Protestant Ethic and the Spirit of Capitalism*, 181.

20. Ernst Troeltsch, *The Social Teaching of the Christian Churches*, trans. Olive Wyon (New York: Harper & Brothers, 1960), 609–10.

which to-day determine the lives of all the individuals who are born into this mechanism ... with irresistible force."[21]

History of the Term "Protestant"

A consideration of the origin of the term "Protestant" provides a basis for the term "protesting" in the labor ethic that will be proposed in this book. Given that the nineteenth-century goal of the "Cooperative Commonwealth" has failed to come true and that the twentieth-century American dream has, for so many, turned into the nightmare of layoffs, plant closings, and diminished expectations for the future, an emphasis on protest is well placed. There is hope if workers unite to collectively take control of their destiny. This is especially true when workers across the world demand a living wage, a harassment-free workplace, and other basic conditions for a more equitable workplace.

Of all workers, Protestant workers might feel a particular solidarity with those who challenge the power of capital and its economic elites. The origin and history of Protestantism suggest that sympathy with those who rise up against authority would be a constitutive aspect of its identity. Of course, this has been true only by exception as most Protestant churches are no different than George Babbitt's stunningly conformist and business-oriented Chatham Road Presbyterian Church in Sinclair Lewis's *Babbitt* (1922).

Yet an account of the emergence of the term "Protestant" suggests other possibilities worth consideration. At the Diet of Worms in 1521, the Holy Roman Empire of the German Nation issued the Edict of Worms to ban the teachings of Martin Luther and his followers. Nevertheless, the spread of the evangelical churches and its reforms continued apace. Though unintended, the first Diet of Speyer (1526) led Lutheran princes and cities to understand that they were granted the authority to carry on religious affairs as they wished. They used the occasion to promote doctrines and practices of the reforming churches. But a new gathering of the estates of the Holy Roman Empire at the second Diet of Speyer (1529) featured a majority of those who would now be called "Catholics." They proceeded to repeal the decision of the first Diet and reinstate the Edict of Worms. This majority voted to restore the for-

---

21. Weber, *The Protestant Ethic and the Spirit of Capitalism*, 181.

mer rights, property, and income of the Roman authorities and religious orders.[22]

The term "protestant" can be traced to the formal protest, or "Protestatio," issued on April 19, 1529, by five territories and fourteen south German cities represented in the Reichstag at the second Diet of Speyer. They declared that they could not and would not consent to the annulment of the freedoms previously accorded to them. They agreed that if the grievances were not addressed by the authorities, then "we herewith PROTEST and testify openly before God, our sole Creator, Preserver, Redeemer and Saviour . . . [and] consider null and void the entire transaction and the intended decree."[23]

One temptation is to read a contemporary understanding of "protest" or "protestation" back into the circumstances of the early sixteenth century. Public and passionate advocacy for or against a given policy or institution is a familiar meaning of protest. The thought that Protestantism at its heart would have such an orientation is encouraging. As a cautionary note, it is important to note that the meaning of the Latin term *protestari* includes "to profess," "declare formally" and to "bear witness openly" and that the later negative connotation "to oppose" or "object to" emerged only later in the seventeenth century.[24] This book intends to hold both senses of the word "protest" for a new "protesting" labor ethic. Workers in the United States need to bear witness to their plight and they also must oppose and object to the conditions that they face.

The use of the term "protest" and an uncritical description of the activities of the "reformers" at the second Diet of Speyer to promote an agenda of protest and agitation in the current day has risk. The Protestant estates of the Holy Roman Empire, the Lutheran princes, and the reformers (especially Luther) were hardly radical advocates of workers' rights to self-determination in their own day.[25] The title of Luther's pam-

---

22. See Kenneth Scott Latourette, *A History of Christianity, Reformation to the Present,* vol. 2 (New York: Harper & Row, 1975), 727; Williston Walker and Richard A. Norris, David W. Lotz, Robert T. Handy, *A History of the Christian Church,* 4th ed. (New York: Charles Scribner's Sons, 1985), 441.

23. "The Protest at Speier," Crozier Theological Seminary Historical Leaflets, no. 1. (Copyright 1901, Henry C. Vedder), 2, 13–14.

24. David W. Lotz, "Protestantism," in *The Oxford Encyclopedia of the Reformation* (New York: Oxford University Press, 1996), 4:352.

25. See Peter Blickle, *The Revolution of 1525: The German Peasants' War from a New Perspective,* trans. Thomas A. Brady Jr. and H. C. Erik Midelfort (Baltimore: Johns Hopkins University Press, 1985).

phlet "Against the Robbing and Murdering Hordes of Peasants" speaks for itself. Nonetheless, it is intriguing to see how the overarching name for the various reformational impulses in the church came about, not from any one of its founders, but as a result of its founding activity. The term "Protestantism" endures. But hardened orthodoxies prevent new practices from responding to the ever curious and surprising exigencies of experience. The reformers who gave rise to the term "Protestant" had their own orthodoxies and unquestioned assumptions. Still, the term serves as an enduring challenge to affirm strongly that "what is" does not always have to be. A challenge will be whether the early transforming power of protest can be brought to bear on the modern workplace in the United States.

Christian ethicists must not stand in the way of agitated and unified workers. A labor ethic that accounts for the interests of laborers and addresses directly the enormous power of capitalism must be developed. Globalization, as such, is not the problem. The issue is who will makes the decisions about the direction of this ongoing, complex, and multi-dimensional phenomenon. Who will benefit and who will lose? The emergence of "global capitalism" and the continued, precipitous decline of the labor movement in the United States suggest that laborers will not be the beneficiaries.

Proponents of the globalization of capitalism glowingly describe the positive economic implications of global capitalism and the worldwide prosperity that is sure to follow. Such are the benefits of regional and global economic organizations like the North American Free Trade Agreement, the World Trade Organization, the World Bank and the International Monetary Fund, and the Free Trade Area of the Americas. Cooperation between corporations and nations on matters ranging from trade to currency policy is the watchword. The world can then be free of the constraining hand of economic nationalism and the dead hand of centralized planning. In this view, the invisible hand is best of all and will lead to and maintain prosperity for everyone.

The issue of labor and management relationships is more important than ever precisely because of the tenuous commitments that corporations make to their employees. The days of lifetime employment are assuredly long past.[26] How long can one keep one's job before it is sent to

---

26. Jackie Krasas Rogers, *Temps: The Many Faces of the Changing Workplace* (Ithaca, N.Y.: Cornell University Press, 2000).

another country or rendered obsolete by advances in technology?[27] Many tout the advantages of the "free market" and the entrepreneurial skills that everyone must acquire to survive in it. The idea that workers should see themselves as "independent contractors" who can move easily from one job to the next is increasingly ascendant. Of course, not everyone fits into this "work model," and it is not surprising that those who support an entrepreneurial orientation to work are themselves entrepreneurs.

Much has been written in the area of Christian business ethics. But an ethic that privileges the insight and outlook of laborers has received scant attention. Ethics, of all disciplines, should be attentive to the daily lived experience of workers. It must enhance, not diminish, the ability of workers to counter the overwhelming control that modern corporations wield with impunity. This book will highlight the positive character of "protest" and "conflict" and offer the possibility that the interests of working-class laborers can be advanced in a more direct fashion. Such an ethic could relegitimate appropriate responses to the constant encroachment of the power of capitalism at the expense of workers. From the perspective of labor, the prevailing neoliberal economic outlook of many contemporary Christian business ethicists is an entirely insufficient resource to address the structural dimensions of problems in the workplace. Most contemporary Christian economic and business ethicists are too timid and too closely identified with managerial interests. Their critiques of capitalist practices are usually limited to suggestions for a "fairer" or more "just" capitalism. Alternatives to capitalism remain unexamined. A willingness to name and advocate workers' interests must become a feature of a new labor ethic.

Summary of the Book

Chapter 2 is an introduction to the world of contemporary labor relations through the story of the Saturn Corporation. Saturn has been trumpeted as a trailblazer in modern labor/management cooperation circles. It has been watched closely by those who ponder what may happen in other corporations who have adopted such practices. The continued preeminence of the automobile industry in this country is such that Saturn

---

27. William M. Adler, *Mollie's Job: A Story of Life and Work on the Global Assembly Line* (New York: Scribner, 2000).

is an important test site for a new way of working and a new way of relating to management specifically and to capital in general.

Chapter 3 will discuss the relationship between contracts and cove-nants, the biblical sources for covenant, and survey examples and appli-cations of covenantal business ethics to the workplace. The covenantal ethical work of Joseph Allen and Stewart Herman will be highlighted to see how they handle the issue of conflict within a covenant. This review of covenantal ethics will serve as an introduction to late nineteenth- and early twentieth-century Protestant calls for cooperation between labor and management in the next chapter.

Chapter 4 examines the war-like relationship between labor and capi-tal after the end of the Civil War through the lens of the Great Strikes of 1877. It also features a brief look at different social gospelers who called for an end to the fighting. Though labor and capital have certainly been at odds since the end of World War II, the struggles in the nineteenth century were recognizable examples of class warfare. The bloody battles between labor and capital during this time prompted social gospel appeals for cooperation. The wish to establish a "Cooperative Commonwealth" resounded through many quarters of society. This chapter will show that contemporary appeals for labor-management cooperation have a long lineage in U.S. Protestantism.

Chapter 5 explores the various attempts to pull labor and manage-ment together since the end of the nineteenth century. A review of company unions, their effects on independent union organizing, and the federal legislation that addresses the organization of unions is intended to situate, historically and legally, contemporary Christian ethical appeals for cooperation, harmony, and stability. Christian business ethicists who support cooperation between managers and workers offer, implicitly and explicitly, powerful justifications for the various employee participation plans, labor-management cooperation programs, quality circles, and the practice of "teamwork" that have been prominent features of the corpo-rate landscape in the United States since the 1970s. This chapter will also include a look at the Teamwork for Employees and Managers Act (TEAM Act) and the ways that employer organizations are trying to weaken historic legislation that protects unions.

Chapter 6 will outline a constructive alternative to a covenantal busi-ness ethic. I will argue that a new "protesting" labor ethic is needed that is unafraid to side with the working class. The basepoints for this protesting labor ethic include the role of imagination to envision new possibilities for laborers, the necessity for labor history, and the commitment to struggle.

•

The use of the word "labor" in this book is intended to effect a much-needed shift in the field of Christian ethics. For all the proposals for a Christian business ethic, and they are legion, rare are the instances when the word "labor" is invoked purposefully. For the most part, Christian social ethicists have neglected an important way to be inclusive. While "labor" could refer to anyone who works, the community to which this project wishes to be held accountable is the working class. I follow Michael Zweig's definition of working class, which includes "those who do the direct work of production and who typically have little control over their jobs and no supervisory authority over others."[28] Such workers comprise 62 percent of the labor force.[29] Of the entire "working-class majority," this book focuses on the experiences of autoworkers in Spring Hill, Tennessee, as a starting point. The hope is that this narrow slice of the working-class experience in the United States will still be recognizable to all workers who have managers and who wonder and worry about the future of their jobs.

---

28. Michael Zweig, *The Working Class Majority: America's Best Kept Secret* (Ithaca, N.Y.: ILR Press, 2000), 34.
29. Ibid.

THE SATURN WORK ETHIC

People don't have any time to do anything but the job. There's no time to breathe, there's no ergonomic relief time.

— Eight-year Saturn veteran[1]

The rolling hills of rural Tennessee seem an unlikely place to formulate a new labor ethic. Yet if one looks carefully among these hills, a massive automobile manufacturing complex emerges amid farmland, antebellum mansions and horse barns. It is at this main location of Saturn Corporation, General Motors' small car automotive division, in the small town of Spring Hill, that a story for the struggle over workers' loyalties, workers' rights, and the conditions of work in the new economy can be told. Behind the carefully constructed landscaping that obscures most of the complex from neighboring Route 31, an ongoing experiment in labor-management relations is unfolding. The results are of great interest to many parties. For its proponents in the automobile industry, the Saturn Corporation is a promising shoot that has poked its way up through the hardened soil of American industry. It has shown that the United States can compete successfully in automobile production where it no longer has unquestioned dominance. Saturn has pulled up to leading Japanese manufacturers with lower costs, greater productivity, and higher standards of quality. For observers of industrial process and industrial relations, Saturn is "the boldest and most far-reaching experiment in organizational form and labor-management relationship created in the last two decades."[2] For Saturn's advocates in the fields of ethics and theology, it exemplifies cooperative workplace practices that emphasize

---

1. Former sixteen-year General Motors employee, name withheld to preserve anonymity, interview by author, tape recording, Spring Hill, Tennessee, August 13, 2000.

2. Saul A. Rubinstein and Thomas A. Kochan, *Learning from Saturn: Possibilities for Corporate Governance and Employee Relations* (Ithaca, N.Y.: ILR Press, 2001), 2.

trust and mutuality rather than adversarial and defensive relationships. One advocate notes that while Saturn has not resolved all its problems, it is still "covenantally viable" and has "covenantal value."[3]

The description to follow of the origin of Saturn provides a sense of the excitement and energy surrounding the vision and the development of this corporation. Despite the near cult status that it has attained in the business press and among Saturn buyers, the final verdict regarding the Saturn experiment can be measured only from the shop floor. What do the workers think and how do they feel about producing Saturn cars on a day-to-day basis? This question is rarely posed but is fundamental to any determination about whether Saturn is, in their terms, "a different kind of company." Or is Saturn merely the same old company for whom the bottom line is the top priority? To find out, this author went to Tennessee and interviewed Saturn workers. Authorized and unauthorized tours of the plant, conversations with workers, and visits to Local 1853's union hall all reveal that Saturn is as odd as the planet its nameplate represents.

Saturn and the New Economy

One way to measure the significance of Saturn is to think of this sub-sidiary of General Motors as an example of "new economy" practices in an "old economy" industry. Many invoke the term "new economy" because it has such a hopeful aura about it. For the champions of the new economy, the old one is redolent of smoke-belching factories, dis-enchanted workers, and trade wars among nations. In the United States, the old economy is synonymous with everything said to be wrong about the 1970s: skyrocketing oil prices, double-digit inflation rates, and plum-meting quality standards. Former President Jimmy Carter summed up these and other aspects of the national condition during his presidency in his famous "malaise" speech.

To what does the new economy refer? It is essential, first of all, to recall the opening of the Berlin Wall in 1989, the breakup of the Warsaw Pact in Eastern Europe, and the dissolution of the U.S.S.R. in 1991. These events opened up the possibility for the worldwide expansion of capitalist enterprises and practices. Mainstream debate is not about the merits of the new economy but about its rate of expansion and the

---

3. Stewart W. Herman, *Durable Goods: A Covenantal Ethic for Management and Employees* (Notre Dame, Ind.: University of Notre Dame Press, 1997), 161.

reach of its practices. An air of historical inevitability pervades most commentary on globalization and the new economy. Francis Fukuyama's "end of history" and the conclusion that "there is no alternative" sums up the mood of triumphant capitalism found in popular and academic reflection on economic questions.[4] In this view, the new economy is the worldwide economy of the 1990s and the new millennium.[5]

A narrower view of the new economy is that it arose from the rapid rise in stock values and the increased number of those who own stock.[6] Another perspective entails a focus on information or "content" and the application of computer technology to every sector of the economy to increase efficiency, productivity, and profitability. The proliferation of Internet-based finance and Internet-based distribution of goods and services has become a beacon of hope. The association of American capitalism with grim images of decaying and rusting factories on the nation's riverways can be forgotten forever in a new economy which is hip, resourceful, and energetic. It is full of momentum with new ideas and the latest technology. It features a youthful workforce and a global economic reach that insures wealth and prosperity for all — or so it is claimed. Organizations such as the World Bank, the World Trade Organization, and the International Monetary Fund help guide the internationalization of the new economy. Agreements such as the North American Free Trade Agreement, Free Trade Area of the Americas, and other regional trade agreements among nations are said to expedite the free and unfettered exchange of goods and services.

The most important aspect of the new economy is the way that work is organized, its content, and the manner in which power relations are expressed. The Saturn Corporation is a new economy landmark for the century-long quest in American industry to find a way to promote cooperation and reduce antagonistic relationships between workers and management. It is an ideal case study to test the claims of contempo-

---

4. See Daniel Singer, *Whose Millennium? Theirs or Ours?* (New York: Monthly Review Press, 1999), 1–2. He notes that "Tina" (There is no alternative — T.I.N.A.) was a nickname for Margaret Thatcher, who often argued for the inevitability of capitalism.

5. There is considerable debate on the meaning of the "new economy." For an excellent short historical summary of the many options, see Jeff Madrick, "Enron, the Media and the New Economy," *The Nation*, April 1, 2002, 17–20. Also Doug Henwood, *A New Economy?* (New York: New Press, forthcoming).

6. Lawrence Mishel, Jared Bernstein, and John Schmitt, *The State of Working America: 2000/2001* (Ithaca, N.Y.: ILR Press, 2001), 19.

rary Christian business ethicists who advocate covenantal relationships between labor and management.

Welcome to Saturn

The $1.9 billion, 4.6 million-square-foot facility in Spring Hill, Tennessee, is a worthy tourist attraction. From horses to horsepower, Saturn lives up to its promotional literature: location is everything. Half of its twenty-four hundred acres is still used as an operating farm growing corn, alfalfa, and hay. The Saturn Welcome Center, adjacent to the main plant, is a converted horse barn — one of the original barns of the Haynes Haven Stock Farm which is the former home of two-time grand champion Tennessee walking horse, Haynes Peacock. The green banners hanging from the rafters of this most unusual horse barn sum up the Saturn ethos. "Saturn is more than a car. It's an idea." "I never say the word 'Saturn' without saying the word team." "Partnership and commitment make anything possible." "We must change in order to survive." "If you can dream it, you can do it."[7]

The short video at the Welcome Center shows wondrous images of a Saturn car winding its way through the Tennessee countryside. Contented workers and congenial managers laboring side by side delight the eye and excite the imagination. A folksy sounding narrator tells the viewer that "GM and the UAW left their baggage behind and started from scratch and began looking at what was right at more than a hundred companies... building a better car begins with building better relationships. No foremen, no time clocks, no us and them, it would be a historic agreement, where everyone would work together in teams, everyone would have a voice, a stake in Saturn's success. What better place for a plant than in a cornfield, a perfect environment for growing things like trust and small town pride."[8]

Saturn's ethos of teamwork and partnership and its promotional emphasis on the agricultural aspects of its location has an uncanny resemblance to Roman mythology. In actuality, the name "Saturn" was

---

7. In succession, the authors are Richard G. "Skip" LeFauve (the first president of Saturn), Roger Smith (former chair of General Motors), Mike Bennett (former president of UAW Local 1853 representing the workers at Saturn), Pearl Bailey, and finally Walt Disney.

8. Author visit to Saturn Welcome Center, The Saturn Corporation, Spring Hill, Tennessee, August 10, 2000.

lifted from the Saturn rocket used to power U.S. space missions, and its corporate logo is drawn from the rings of the planet. Yet the connection of the car's name with the Roman god Saturn and the "Saturnalia" — the most important festival of the agricultural season in the Roman calendar — is unexpectedly apropos. Slaves were allowed to participate in this festival. One notable feature included a role reversal when slaves would issue commands and masters had to obey.[9] In another account of the days at the Saturnalia festival, the "Golden Age" returns to Earth. "No war could be then declared; slaves and masters ate at the same table; executions were postponed; it was a season for giving presents; it kept alive in men's minds the idea of equality, of a time when all were on the same level."[10] The idea of "eating at the same table" and "equality" is part of the Saturn Corporation mythology today of "A Different Kind of Company. A Different Kind of Car." Union employees and salaried managers even share a cafeteria — not a usual sight at most car factories around the country.

Conventional accounts of Saturn's history begin in 1982 with engineering concerns. In that year, a group of engineers and designers gathered at General Motors to dream up a new small car that could compete successfully with the growing popularity of Japanese automobiles.[11] They decided that only a completely new way of manufacturing a car could challenge Japan's growing reputation for quality production and its continued market share advances. Their study concluded that GM had the technology to produce the car in a competitive way. Yet from a labor relations perspective, competitiveness would be impossible.[12] In 1983, Al Warren (vice president of industrial relations for GM) approached Don Ephlin of the UAW (director of the GM Department) and asked if the UAW would be interested in working together on the design and development of this completely new product. According to Ephlin, the answer was overwhelmingly affirmative. "As union leaders we of the UAW had a great interest in saving jobs and becoming competitive without reducing the members' standard of living."[13]

9. Jo Forty, *Mythology: A Visual Encyclopedia* (London: PRC Publishing, 1999), 322.

10. Edith Hamilton, *Mythology: Timeless Tales of Gods and Heroes* (New York: Meridian, 1989), 45.

11. For specific details on the inception of Saturn, see Joe Sherman, *In the Rings of Saturn* (New York: Oxford University Press, 1994), 77–78.

12. Jack O'Toole, *Forming the Future: Lessons from the Saturn Corporation* (Cambridge, Mass.: Blackwell Publishers, 1996), 5.

13. Donald F. Ephlin, foreword, in ibid., vii.

The original idea envisioned a committee of six people to study how to manage this new project. At Ephlin's urging, the UAW advocated that this number be expanded. General Motors agreed, and in February 1984, the historic "Group of 99" met for the first time in Detroit. General Motors managers and staff personnel from fifty-five GM plants and forty-one UAW locals were represented on this planning group. A steering committee handed them the assignment to "integrate people and technology to manufacture small cars in the United States."[14] By May 1984, the group had put in over fifty thousand hours of study and two million miles of travel for the purpose of learning from forty-nine General Motors plants and sixty benchmark companies around the world.[15]

All who cared about Saturn's future knew that they had to surpass decisively two barriers facing the U.S. automobile industry as a whole and General Motors in particular. The first was the mounting evidence and widespread assumption that U.S. automobile manufacturers could not outdesign, outbuild, and outsell Japanese small car imports. The second was the apparent permanence of adversarial relationships between union and management. Saturn was determined to change that dynamic by integrating people, technology, and business systems. This Saturn "trinity" understands heresy as any doctrine or practice that upholds one dimension of the corporation to the exclusion of the others. All three systems must be present at every phase of automobile production. Labor and management are jointly responsible to insure this outcome. Business systems, not usually the concern of labor, had to become part of labor's portfolio. In turn, management became obligated to tend to "people concerns." Advanced technology would carry forth both labor and management into a bright future. In the words of one of Saturn's official tour guides:

> GM knew they had to do something different, and pretty dramatic. They partnered up with the UAW, which is something they're not used to doing. They were pretty much sworn enemies at the time; they put together a group of people to go out and benchmark successful companies and try and figure out what they did right.

14. O'Toole, *Forming the Future*, 6.

15. Richard G. LeFauve and Arnoldo C. Hax, "Saturn — The Making of the Modern Corporation," in *Globalization, Technology, and Competition: The Fusion of Computers and Telecommunications in the 1990s*, ed. Stephen P. Bradley, Jerry A. Hausman, and Richard L. Nolan (Boston: Harvard Business School Press, 1993), 257–81. Also see O'Toole, *Forming the Future*, 18–19.

When they all got back together, they all came up with pretty much one thing: that if you trust and respect your employees, they'll give you that trust and respect back. This is Saturn.

The Memorandum of Agreement

The vehicle for insuring this outcome is the "Memorandum of Agreement." This is the name of the "contract" between Saturn management and the workers represented by Local 1853 of the United Auto Workers. It is an exception to the National Agreement that covers unionized GM employees everywhere else in the United States. The Memorandum is intended to actualize the Saturn values, and it far exceeds what General Motors and the United Auto Workers ever thought was permissible or possible in terms of contractual flexibility.

Jack O'Toole, an original member of the "Group of 99," Saturn's study and planning committee, described the promise of the Memorandum in this way:

The stark reality of the depth of animosity between the adversaries shone as it never had in the past before the hawk eyes of these agents of change. The distrust and disdain for each other, having never been addressed over the last five decades, had taken form in voluminous verbiage with all the tones of parent (GM) talking to child (UAW) and the human characteristic of, "Tell me how far I can go, so I can figure out how to go farther without being caught."[16]

The National Agreement is a remarkable document. Weighing in at over six hundred pages, it covers an encyclopedic array of topics related to the automobile production process and the workplace. The table of contents alone reaches nearly twenty pages. General Motors' introduction to this highly detailed portrait of the state of labor management relations at the end of the 1990s is rife with innuendo about the difficulties faced in the past:

General Motors holds that the basic interests of employers and employees are the same. However, at times employees and the management have different ideas on various matters affecting their

---

16. O'Toole, *Forming the Future*, 50.

relationship. The management of General Motors is convinced that there is no reason why these differences cannot be peacefully and satisfactorily adjusted by sincere and patient effort on both sides.[17]

O'Toole reports that the planning process for the Memorandum of Agreement was a "wonder of synergy," which happened when traditionally opposing parties agreed to an alternative that occurred through working together. "The brilliance of picking out the lack of mutual or individual commitments in the traditional agreement, and then making respective commitments the cornerstones of the memo...was the 'breakwith' thinking that allowed Saturn to crest every monstrous wave of resistance it faced in those crucial forming years."[18] The document had to be "cloaked in vagueness to effectively deal with change; ambiguous enough not to be overtly constricting and with flexibility built into its very core so that if the wrong decisions were made, with the best intentions, they could be quickly addressed and rectified without waiting for an expiration date."[19]

There were several guiding considerations in constructing this Memorandum. The partnered group needed to find a way to write a contract that would honor over a half century of collective bargaining built into the GM/UAW National Agreement and not merely repeat most or all of its encyclopedic reach. They also had to "make sure that the respective commitments of the parties, or lack of commitments, were not merely matched in the memo, but understood so well that the Saturn Agreement could not be challenged in any way as being inferior."[20] In sum, General Motors and the United Auto Workers had to trust each other enough to let go of the assurances that detailed contracts provide. Known around the Saturn plant as the "grey book," the Memorandum is a pocket-sized document just short of forty pages in length. It is a groundbreaking document because of its brevity and the omission of the usual Management Rights Clause. This clause, "Paragraph 8," is central to the National Agreement that governs GM and UAW relationships. It stipulates the exclusive rights of GM which include the "right to hire;

---

17. Introduction, *Agreement between UAW and the General Motors Corporation*, November 2, 1996.

18. O'Toole, *Forming the Future*, 51.

19. Ibid., 48.

20. Ibid., 50.

promote; discharge or discipline for cause; and to maintain discipline and efficiency of employees." In addition, "the products to be manufactured, the location of the plants, the schedules of production, the methods, processes, and means of manufacturing are solely and exclusively the responsibility of the Corporation."[21]

O'Toole's humorous assessment of the National Contract is that "it didn't take a calculus professor to figure out that 80 percent of this large agreement consisted of exceptions to that tiny Paragraph 8."[22] Yet it has been the exceptions and the details that have guided, in fine detail over hundreds of pages, the relationship between GM management and its unionized autoworkers in the United States. Even without the customary language, there is no question that the GM/UAW Memorandum of Agreement is a contract. Yet it leaves much to the outcomes of workers' daily lived experience of the Saturn values. The openness to change and the extraordinary flexibility inherent in this contract sets Saturn apart.

Instead of merely designating management as the final arbiter of all decisions relating to the manufacturing process, the Memorandum of Agreement stipulates full participation by the union and the use of a consensus decision-making process. In theory, placement of authority and decision making is not necessarily vested in management. It is supposed to be assigned to the "most appropriate part of the organization, with emphasis on the Work Unit; and, free flow of information and clear definition of the decision-making process."[23] The "Group of 99" insisted that the Saturn concept be a partnership on all levels. The partnership between union and management would be expressed in the design of the car, its manufacture, and the way it would be sold. Owen Bieber, then president of the UAW, noted that the effort to write the contract and agree upon it represented "a degree of co-determination never before reached in U.S. collective bargaining."[24]

---

21. Paragraph 8, *Agreement between UAW and the General Motors Corporation*, November 2, 1996, 13.

22. O'Toole, *Forming the Future*, 51.

23. *Memorandum of Agreement: Saturn and the U.A.W.*, 2000, section 10, "Structure and Decision-Making Guidelines," 5.

24. Sherman, *In the Rings of Saturn*, 86. Despite this enthusiastic endorsement, Bieber did take the effort to note in a letter attached to the Memorandum of Agreement dated July 23, 1985, that "the UAW considers the proposed Memorandum of Agreement as a 'special case' because it is specifically designed as an integral part of the Saturn approach. Therefore, the UAW does not consider this Memorandum of Agreement as a precedent regarding the Union's policy at any other facility, including those at General Motors" (41).

In December 1999, a companion grey booklet to the Memorandum of Agreement was issued. Entitled "Guiding Principles," it expresses the "Saturn morality" in very clear terms. On the very first page, everyone is called upon to "look forward to the decades ahead" and "recommit" to Saturn's five shared values, which are "fundamental to all Saturn Team Members." The Guiding Principles booklet entreats everyone to support these values through their behavior. Everyone must "walk the talk," which includes the commitment to customer enthusiasm, commitment to excel, teamwork, trust and respect for each other, and continuous improvement. Customer enthusiasm entails exceeding expectations in cost, quality, and satisfaction. Customers must know that Saturn "really cares about them." The second value repudiates mediocrity and half-hearted efforts and defines excellence as "reaching beyond the best" by accepting responsibility, accountability, and authority for overcoming any obstacle. The third value, teamwork, entails singleness of purpose and the belief that individual talents can flourish while still maintaining team growth. Trust and respect for the individual, the fourth value, includes a recognition of what is unique in every person. A team made up of such individuals can build confidence and creativity and achieve a high degree of initiative, self-respect, and self-discipline. The fifth value, continuous improvement, means that at all times, the quality, cost, and effectiveness of all products and services must be improved. The sustained success of Saturn depends upon the practice of this fifth value.

The Guiding Principles nudges the Saturn workers closer to the GM/UAW National Agreement. Even though it is very short at sixty-eight pages, it does spell out the compensation and benefits package for Saturn workers as well as the attendance policy. The Guiding Principles grey book describes what in other contexts would be termed the disciplinary process. Saturn prefers to view it as the "consultation process," which counsels, guides, and reviews "members" or workers so that they can live up to the responsibility and accountability that every Saturn worker must have to contribute to the team. An extensive process is outlined that places the accent on "help" as opposed to "punishment" and "constructive instruction," not "discipline." This includes three formal steps. The first is the Amber Zone, in which a member is reminded of Saturn's mission, philosophy and shared values. This is intended to help the member contribute to the goals of Saturn. If this does not occur, a member moves to the Red Zone, and a new, formal, written corrective action plan is formulated. The final level is "Decision Day," when a member has an inadequate response in the Red Zone. The member is excused for three days, with pay, to enable the member to discern whether to continue employment with Saturn. At each level, the Saturn member has both management and leaders in the UAW available for representation and consultation.

Many workers joke about the color of the books precisely because there are so many grey areas in the contract. The "grey areas" are not accidental but intended to make the contract a "living document." Under other contracts, modifications of work arrangements might have to wait for the negotiations involved at contract renewal time. Not so at Saturn. Procedures for consensus building are outlined in the grey books so that decisions and disagreements can be resolved jointly and in a timely way between the company and the union. "Resolution is achieved through the joint efforts of the parties in discovering the 'best' solution. The solution must provide a high level of acceptance for all parties.... Any of the parties may block a potential decision. However, the party blocking the decision must search for alternatives. In the event an alternative solution is not forthcoming, the blocking party must reevaluate the position in the context of the philosophy and mission."[25] This is intended to encompass the entire structure of the Saturn operation, from the president to each line worker.

The perspective of Saturn's first president, Richard "Skip" G. LeFauve, provides a fascinating insight into management's early hopes for Saturn. "Partnership" is his one-word summary for Saturn culture. Calling it the "clean sheet" approach, the overall goal is to create a new environment that would develop a "close partnership between the UAW and GM, which would involve union leadership in all managerial decisions of a strategic, tactical, and operational nature."[26] For LeFauve, the partnership consists of two overlapping circles. Most, but not all, decisions fall into this overlap area. The goal is to help the two groups become more comfortable with each other and narrow the gap between management and union roles. A strategic planning process is employed to bring union and management together and to reeducate them about each other's respective roles. This educational process will help "union

---

25. *Memorandum of Agreement: Saturn and the U.A.W., 2000*, section 11, "Consensus Guidelines," 10–11.

26. LeFauve and Hax, "Saturn — The Making of the Modern Corporation," 262.

leaders to become more business-oriented and managers to understand how employees at all levels feel about the business and its direction."[27]

Saturn announced the completed contract and the site for the manufacture of the first Saturns in July 1985. Five years later, then GM chairman Roger B. Smith and then UAW president Owen Bieber drove the very first Saturn car, a red four-door sedan, off the assembly line. This location in the plant where cars come off the line to be shipped around the world is called Inspiration Point. A sign on the shop floor says that it is "the shipping point for the world's best cars." Since then, Saturn has become a fixture on the road and in the hearts of its owners. Customer satisfaction is reflected in the Saturn Car Clubs that have sprouted up around the country. The Car Clubs have a credo that convey a sense of the Saturn culture. "I drive a different kind of car. From a different kind of car company. Which makes me a different kind of person. I don't just care about my car, I care about my community. Caring more about people than parts is something I share with other Saturn owners. That's why I belong to the Car Club. And the Car Club belongs to me. You're not just in the club, you are the club."[28] The communitarian sensibility of Saturn can also be observed in their well-attended "homecomings." Since the 1990s, tens of thousands of enthusiastic customers have driven their Saturns back to the birthplace of their car, in Spring Hill, to have picnics and concerts under big top tents and get pictures taken with workers.

Saturn Work Ethic and Membership

One way to summarize the Saturn work ethic is to recall the five values of commitment to customer enthusiasm, excellence, teamwork, trust and respect for the individual, and continuous improvement. These values *are* the "Saturn morality." While Saturn deems them values, one might also see them as the Saturn virtues. They are virtues because they are to be the outcome of work habits brought to practiced perfection. The values are meant to become second nature to each worker. Not everyone is inclined or able to embody the Saturn morality. At the beginning, the most pressing matter for Saturn was to identify and recruit workers who were open to a wholehearted embrace of this ethic.

27. Ibid., 263.
28. From a display at the Saturn Welcome Center (August 2000).

Since Saturn built an entirely new plant in Tennessee, one might expect they would hire fresh, eager, and energetic young workers who
would be receptive to the whole Saturn ethos. Much to the disap-
pointment of would-be car builders in the Spring Hill area, the UAW
stipulated that laid off or at-risk workers in GM plants across the country
be given the first chance to sign up. It is likely that officials at GM viewed
this as a significant concession on their part since they were unsure that
workers from the "old world" of traditional GM-UAW adversarialism
could be changed to embrace the "new world" of labor management partnerships. As one observer put the problem, the UAW prospects "already
had a good dose of the old world, with its work rules, grievance procedures, and time clocks, as well as occasional in-plant sabotage, alcohol
and drug abuse, and an often distressing indifference to quality."[29]

To deal with the hiring process, Saturn put together its Recruiting,
Application, Screening, and Selection department (RASS) in 1988. This
hiring campaign began in a GM plant in Willow Springs, Illinois. RASS
representatives eventually toured 136 UAW-affiliated GM plants in an
extensive outreach program to recruit both active and laid-off UAW
members. The applicants endured an extensive screening, interview, and
orientation process.[30] The screening process for potential Saturn members was a matter of measuring will, desire, and eagerness. This was
accomplished by a phone call that lasted nearly an hour using a standard script to grade and assess readiness for working at Saturn — to see
where a worker's "mind was at."[31] Once a potential member passed the
phone interview, an on-site visit became the next step. Saturn actually
paid for the airline tickets, the hotel costs, and other expenses for potential members to visit the plant and the area. A tour of the Spring Hill
plant and interviews with both GM and UAW "advisors" from various
work modules were conducted. Tests in math, reading, and problem solving were scheduled. In the initial hiring phase, the introductory phone
interviews yielded one out of three applicants. Of the pool that made it
to Spring Hill, one in five was selected and offered a job. Upon accepting
a job at Saturn, one officially becomes a "team member."

To be hired was not the only hoop separating a worker from the line.
When the first Saturns started rolling off the assembly lines in 1990,

---

29. Sherman, *In the Rings of Saturn,* 171.
30. Ibid., 170.
31. Ibid., 195.

nearly a million hours had been invested in training the original three thousand Saturn workers. Each individual worker went through 300–350 hours of instruction to gain familiarity with all the tasks of the team. Also, new hires had to undergo "Saturn Awareness Training," which inculcated the mission and philosophy of Saturn. Some workers refer to "Awareness" as another word for becoming "Saturnized." To maintain this enormous investment, 5 percent of the original forty-hour work weeks in the early 1990s was allocated to additional non-production-oriented educational work. Saturn wanted every worker to make the mental transition from an individualistic sensibility to the collective orientation necessary to the entire operation. Educated workers must be part of actualized, self-directed production teams accountable to each other. They cannot be dependent on outside sources of authority for the power to complete the job.[32]

The Saturn People Philosophy is an important statement of the Saturn work ethic. "We believe that all people want to be involved in decisions that affect them, care about their jobs and each other, take pride in themselves and in their contributions and want to share in the success of their efforts." The extraordinary way that Saturn recognizes the collective adherence to this philosophy is found in the "Job Security" section.

> Saturn recognizes that people are the most valuable asset of the organization. It is people who develop new technologies and systems, and people who make these systems work in order to meet Saturn's mission. Accordingly, those Saturn members who are eligible for job security … shall not be laid off except in situations which the SAC [Strategic Action Council] determines are due to unforeseen or catastrophic events or severe economic conditions. … Saturn recognizes the desirability of regular employment and will attempt to avoid laying off members not eligible for job security.[33]

---

32. Sherman, *In the Rings of Saturn*, 196–98. The details of the hiring and training process are a summary of Sherman's research. The comment on "Awareness" and becoming "Saturnized" is from an on-site interview by the author with a Saturn employee (August 12, 2000). The Saturn ethos seems to persist despite criticisms that the original ardor for training and education has cooled off in recent years.

33. *Memorandum of Agreement: Saturn and the U.A.W.*, 2000, section 21, "Job Security," 16–17.

Workers who came to Saturn from General Motors plants around the country where layoffs were a way of life viewed this clause as a stunning departure from the "old world." It took some of the sting out of the arduous relocation to Tennessee. For a job situation that was not at the outset much more than an experiment, such a guarantee was an incentive to take a chance on Saturn.

The Structure of Work at Saturn

The most arresting image in the packet prepared for visitors to the Saturn Welcome Center is the one that shows the difference between traditional work hierarchies and the work arrangement at Saturn. This is captured by two images. The first is a triangle; the second is a circle. Inside the triangle there is a figure of a single person standing on the shoulders of two people, with those two people standing on three people, and so on until a pyramid is formed. The second image is made up of concentric circles with people arranged in all of the circles with no one person apparently in charge of anyone else. There is no obvious order except that of the circles radiating out from the center. The circles capture the essence of the Saturn Corporation. The training at Saturn, call it awareness or becoming "Saturnized," is about enabling workers to operate outside that triangle.

While the circle expresses the conceptual vision of work at Saturn, there is an assembly line with individual workers who attend to what arrives from another point on the line. But assembly-line workers do not respond primarily to supervisors but to other members of the team. Each worker or "work unit member" is part of a "work unit," which is an "integrated group" of approximately eight to twelve workers.

The work units are the teams that form the core of the Saturn operation. Each unit has its own individual team center within the Saturn plant. A tour guide (a production worker who rotated out of his team for a short period to do public relations work) made the following comments:

> These white buildings on the inside are the team centers. Each team has one, and they are encouraged to decorate the team centers any way they want. Any UT fans here? You can see someone is. They painted their team center the University of Tennessee orange and white. Those team centers contain a computer, printer for record keeping, a TV and VCR for training, tables and chairs

to make the breaks a little easier, refrigerator, microwave.... This is like their own little business within a bigger business.[34]

The organizational structure of Saturn builds off the work unit. The work unit counselor (WUC) for each team is a member of the union and performs tasks similar to those of a nonunion foreman in another setting. The counselor's overall main goal is to promote the Saturn partnership in the team. In cooperation with the team, priorities and goals are established. These are met by the management of daily production, quality, and costs. Job certifications, job rotation, conflict management between team members, training, housekeeping, and safety issues are all aspects of the work unit counselor's extensive portfolio. Communication with other work units is necessary. Finally, counselors must take advantage of Saturn resources to nurture team growth and development so that teams become self-managed work units. Each work unit counselor is expected to work on the line for a substantial portion of the day in addition to fulfilling duties as a counselor. If a member of the work unit or team is unable to work or is not at work, this is a problem that the work unit counselor must solve. Sometimes this entails working on the line the entire day. Off-line duties remain but are deferred to another day. For these efforts, the counselor is not paid any additional wages.

Two or more work units form a work unit module if their tasks need to be coordinated or if they are geographically related. Work unit modules have UAW and management advisors called Operations Module Advisors. At the next level of organization, work unit modules come together to form a business unit. In the factory at Spring Hill, there are three business units, which cover the three fundamental aspects of Saturn automobile production: engine/transmission, the body of the car, and assembly (powertrain, body systems, vehicle systems, respectively). The Manufacturing Action Council (MAC) oversees the three business units. The president of the UAW local representing the workers at Saturn (Local 1853) is on the MAC as is Saturn's vice president of manufacturing. Overseeing this and other councils is the Strategic Action Council (SAC), which is responsible for the "strategic business planning necessary to assure the long-term viability of the enterprise and will be responsive to the needs of the marketplace relative to quality, cost, and

---

34. Comments of tour guide, Saturn tour by author, tape recording, Spring Hill, Tennessee, August 9, 2000.

timing. The SAC will obtain, maintain, and replace the resources necessary to meet the mission in concert with the philosophy. It is charged
with creating the environment, facilities, tools, education, and support
systems which will enable Saturn members to perform their responsibilities."[35] This highest decision-making body has a union member on it. At
every level of the Saturn manufacturing operation, the corporate goal is
to seek both UAW and management input and representation.

The point that each team and its center is a business within a larger
business is a good way to describe the thirty functions for which each
work unit, as a whole, is responsible. The functions range from concepts about work at Saturn to some very specific tasks. Whatever the
function, they are intended to actualize the team concept. Nonetheless,
the workers in these work units or teams have an enormous amount of
responsibility relative to the assembly-line jobs that they left behind in
GM plants around the country. The thirty functions may be grouped
into roughly four broad categories.

The first category includes the foundational functions that are necessary to become a team. They include consensus decision making,
self-direction, job planning and assignment, conflict resolution, commitment to synergistic group growth and "consultative procedures for
self-corrective action." In sum, the team has mastered these functions if
it is able to fulfill work goals without relying upon outside authorities —
management — to direct and supervise each step of the work process. In
sum, leadership rotation within a team that practices group consensus
is the best approach to identify the required work and to accomplish it
through win-win solutions for all team members. Any individual member can stop a decision if that member is able to point to a reasonable
alternative. Consensus is present if all team members are 70 percent
comfortable with a decision and have 100 percent commitment to the
implementation of the decision. A team has achieved synergy if it has
attained a state where "the team" is greater than the sum of each of
its individual members. A clear understanding of team goals and the
ability to enhance group knowledge and effectiveness are the steps toward synergy. Finally, the "consultative procedure" is the team approach
alternative to discipline that used to be administered by foremen and
supervisors from the "old world." The intent is for the team to take re-

35. *Memorandum of Agreement: Saturn and the U.A.W., 2000*, section 10, "Structure and Decision-Making Process," 10.

sponsibility to establish and ensure "behavioral norms consistent with the concepts of Saturn's mission, philosophy, and shared value system."

The second category of functions pertains to personnel and training issues within the team. The team is to schedule and hold its own meetings as a result of its developing understanding of what is needed "to run their part of the business." The team has the responsibility to schedule vacations for the team members, plan relief and break times during any given workday, and provide replacements for unscheduled absentees. Selection decisions about hiring new members must be in accordance with the team's determination of the person power necessary for that team's range of responsibility. Teams or work units are responsible for the performance of their own health and safety programs. Finally, the teams are to identify training needs and use available resources in Saturn to ensure that they consist of "world-class automotive workers."

The functions discussed so far point inward toward the team and its members. The third category of functions points outward to the material preconditions for building automobiles. These include a control of scrap and inventory, budgeting, and the performance of equipment maintenance. The team orders and obtains supplies and resources and performs housekeeping and cleaning in its work area. One worker described the purchase decisions ranging from "brooms to million-dollar equipment." Thus, the need for scrupulous record keeping ensures that everyone remains responsible and accountable to each member in the team and to the rest of Saturn.

The fourth category of functions includes activities to enhance inter-team communications within the Saturn plant. While the teams are responsible for designing their own jobs and determining the methods to carry out those jobs, they are also accountable to other teams and their production and personnel needs. This is referred to as "horizontal integration." Communication networks within the team and the communications links between teams throughout the Saturn plant are vital. This network makes it possible for teams to "perform their own repairs." This is a major difference between Saturn and many other automobile plants. At Saturn, "customers" also include the next person or team further down the assembly line. If work is not done according to specification by one team, it is not the responsibility of the next team to fix the mistakes. The work must be sent back to the team that produced the mistake. The point is to do the job correctly the first time to avoid the accumulation of subsidiary problems that inevitably follow. This enables all the workers and the teams to fulfill the Saturn value of continuous improvement in quality, cost, and work environment.

Once a member is in a given team, then that worker becomes directly accountable to a family of related, but distinct, car building tasks that are completed on a rotating basis. Workers at Saturn do not simply come in, punch in at the clock, and hope for the best. In fact, they do not punch in at all. They report to the team center to meet with fellow team members to discuss the work of the previous shift and to map out the work for their own shift. The expectation level for engagement and involvement in each worker's job is very high. The requirement to know all of the work tasks in one's team so as to efficiently carry out the job rotation has an important advantage from the standpoint of production. A worker who is sick, on restriction, or on vacation can be replaced instantly in this type of work organization no matter the complexity of a given task. Ongoing off-line training ensures that these workers continue to build skills.

Pitfalls of the Team Concept

Job rotation is a component of the teamwork concept and a difficult fact of the work life at Saturn. In the words of a ten-year veteran of Saturn: "The most important way about teamwork is that we rotate our jobs. Each member of the team, there's thirteen of us, will do each job. We can structure it any way we want to, we can rotate it on a daily basis, hourly, quarterly, my team rotates every half hour."[36] When asked about a typical workday at Saturn, another worker reported, "First thing, I go into my team center and see who's there and who's not there, and then figure out what job we're going to start at; we usually rotate through jobs, so I would get my starting point and then go through the day going from job to job doing different procedures."[37]

Job rotation is designed to ensure that workers do not suffer the physical and mental fatigue of repeating one task for ten hours a day (the now typical workday length at Saturn). This is one positive aspect of rotation. Workers at Saturn do have pride in the quality of their work. But Saturn workers are keenly aware of the pitfalls of teamwork and job

36. Former Fiero plant (GM, Michigan) employee, name withheld to preserve anonymity, interview by author, tape recording, Spring Hill, Tennessee, August 9, 2000.

37. Former GM worker, Tarrytown, New York, name withheld to preserve anonymity, interview by author, tape recording, Spring Hill, Tennessee, August 12, 2000.

rotation. When one tour guide was asked about the difficulties with the team concept after a tour of the plant, he replied:

> Any difficulties? Oh, yeah, there's plenty of difficulties with that; the team I was in had ten people, and everybody has their own opinion on how to do things. A lot of the votes to do the things we wanted to do came down to 51–49, because everyone can see both sides of the issue. Yeah, there are difficulties, it's not a quick way to do things, but it's the best way to do things, because if everyone buys into it, then everyone will do it. But if you get one person who says "No, I ain't gonna do it!" — then what can you do?[38]

In addition to the problems of consensus, the size of a given team as it relates to the assigned tasks is a pressing concern. One difficulty is when a team member is absent, sick, or on restriction. There is no set rule for every group of tasks that a replacement must be found. Teams sometimes have to make adjustments that either speed up everyone's work or eliminate (for a given shift or even days or weeks at a time) less demanding off-line duties. In still other situations, the teams are "rebalanced." This occurs when a team is deemed too large for its assigned tasks. The team size contracts and again, in many situations, off-line functions suffer, training is decreased, and workers bear more of the physical brunt of the day-to-day manufacturing process. Though millions of dollars were invested in the most up-to-date ergonomic innovations at Saturn, there are still many tasks that require heavy lifting and the arduous manipulation of power tools. Nearly all of the jobs are fully "loaded." Tasks are timed to be started and completed with virtually no break in between. One worker in the general assembly area complained that Saturn "wants 95 percent productivity, 95 percent of the time you're going to be doing something on that car. . . . I have seen people who have no time to blow their nose on the line, that is no joke."[39]

When there is a downturn in the market, there is no need to produce as many cars. The speed of the assembly line does slow down. But the opposite of what one might expect occurs. On the assembly line in the powertrain area (engine and transmission assembly), instead of less work, there is more "time" to work. Thus, instead of building one part, a person

---

38. Comments of tour guide, Saturn tour by author, tape recording, Spring Hill, Tennessee, August 9, 2000.

39. Former seven-year General Motors employee, name withheld to preserve anonymity, interview by author, tape recording, Spring Hill, Tennessee, August 12, 2000.

can now build two parts. In powertrain, a worker not only builds a part, but stocks the job as well. With each new part assembly, a worker must be responsible for additional stock work. This involves walking away from the line to open "dunnage" or the black crates in which the materials arrive. Yet only the amount of time in which one works on the line itself counts in the time studies. One extra part assembly does not look like a major issue until one considers that the "dunnage" work is doubled. As one powertrain worker put it: "You take more steps to assemble the product and you never get ahead because the line never stops. There is not much room for a dropped nut or any kind of mistake."[40] This type of productivity optimization is an example of the fifth value, continuous improvement, in action.

Continuous improvement is a double-edged phenomenon. On the one hand, it is hard to argue with an ergonomic innovation that reduces lifting and stress in any given production task. An innovation that improves the quality of the product always sounds like a good idea. Yet continuous improvement also entails "improving" one's work. The constant concern is how to be more efficient and reduce "wasted" movement and "wasted" time. If more work is forced into every minute for every worker, throughout the plant, job elimination can occur. The number of workers on a team can be "rebalanced." This is Saturn-speak for the reality that, most of the time, a rebalanced team is a team that suffers a reduction in the number of team members. A worker could be sent to another team. If a worker resigns from Saturn, that worker is simply not replaced.

At Saturn, like everywhere else, building automobiles is not an easy job.[41] In a case brought to the United States Court of Appeals for the Sixth Circuit, a jury found in favor of the plaintiff in *Ronald Jeffrey Kiphart v. Saturn Corporation.*[42] Kiphart, a UAW worker at Saturn, sued Saturn and the UAW under the Americans with Disabilities Act (ADA) after

---

40. Former twenty-four-year GM employee, name withheld to preserve anonymity, interview by author, e-mail communication, January 26, 2002.

41. For perspectives on work at GM automotive plants, see *Ben Hamper's Rivethead: Tales from the Assembly Line* (New York: Warner Books, 1986) and Solange De Santis, *Life on the Line: One Woman's Tale of Work, Sweat, and Survival* (New York: Anchor Books, 1999). Laurie Graham went to work for Subaru-Izuzu Automotive and tells the story in *On the Line at Subaru-Izuzu: The Japanese Model and the American Worker* (Ithaca, N.Y.: ILR Press, 1995).

42. *Ronald Jeffrey Kiphart v. Saturn Corporation,* USCA6 Opinion 01a0178p.06 (6th Cir. 2001).

he was removed from his work team for tendonitis and a herniated disk. After a series of temporary jobs at Saturn, he was put on involuntary medical leave for seven months. The case was based on the allegation that Saturn did not follow its own rules that stipulate job rotation for all of the production jobs. While Kiphart was out on involuntary medical leave, other disabled employees were allowed to work without having to do the required job rotation. Kiphart's case was originally part of a broader lawsuit brought by seventy-seven Saturn employees that alleged race, age, and sex discrimination as well as disability discrimination under the ADA.

In this case, Saturn did not follow its own contract. Repeated attempts to deal with workplace injuries at Saturn in a context that has largely foregone the use of the grievance procedure as a means to leverage management into doing the right thing has resulted in an even more demanding work environment. Unlike other unionized automobile plants, Saturn workers lack the instruments to fairly adjudicate situations such as these.

Work Life at Saturn and UAW Local 1853

The delegation to the average worker of certain levels of authority and decision-making power once held exclusively by management is the essence of the Saturn system. Saturn grants just enough authority to empower workers but withholds enough so that the corporation maintains effective control of the entire operation. The Saturn rhetoric conveys the ideal that the workers, through the union, were involved from the design stage to the way cars would be sold. But the ultimate decisions about the ownership of Saturn itself, capital investment decisions, and the relationship of Saturn to General Motors remain well outside the scope of the union's power. The bottom line is that even though the famed Paragraph 8, or management rights clause, is absent in the Saturn contract, it is still operative in an unofficial manner at Saturn.

In interviews with Saturn workers, the difficulties of the Saturn-UAW partnership were expressed in a number of ways. A twenty-five-year veteran at the GM plant in Framingham, Massachusetts, and a Saturn worker for six years reported that an early commercial for Saturn featured a UAW member and a management person walking together toward a motel. While I was not able to independently confirm the content of this commercial, the hilarious perception that the Saturn partnership could be summed up as a motel tryst is quite telling. Reportedly, the commercial was dropped soon thereafter because of the impolite comparisons being drawn between the hallowed partnership and activities in a Motel 6. In connection with his comments about the commercial, he noted "UAW leaders do more for a member of management that passed away than they ever would do for their union brothers and sisters."[43] The leadership of the UAW identified more with their management counterparts than they did with the rank-and-file workers who elected them. While this is not an unfamiliar scenario in American unionism, the sense is that the problem is more pronounced at Saturn.

The partnership has also caused difficulties among the workers themselves. Another long-time veteran of GM harbored deep suspicions about the teamwork concept. "I think that this labor-management relation concept, in reality, pits workers against workers. In the old world, you worked together and respected each other as UAW workers, you were all UAW workers, there was management and there was the union, and there was a clearly defined line. The line has been crossed over and blurred so that UAW workers want to achieve greater heights than they had before. They want to get on the good side of management and in doing so will lose their loyalty and respect for the individual they are working beside."[44]

Within the context of the work unit, workers are presented with the broad parameters of the tasks to be accomplished. They are then left to figure out how to accomplish these tasks in concert with their work unit counselor and, at times, other union officials at different levels of the production process. Management is not absent from these proceedings. It is present but not to scold, prod, or otherwise force workers to perform. Instead, management serves as a partner-facilitator to guide tasks to completion and problems toward solutions. Workers have to work together as a team and hold each accountable as they seek out solutions. As more than one worker noted, this requires a "mature" labor force to succeed. While this may be true, the real issue is that workers are forced to internalize, within their teams, problems that may not be of their own making. The negative result is that union members become distracted

---

43. Former Framingham employee, name withheld to preserve anonymity, interview by author, tape recording, Spring Hill, Tennessee, August 10, 2000.

44. Former GM worker, Tarrytown, New York, name withheld to preserve anonymity, interview by author, tape recording, Spring Hill, Tennessee, August 12, 2000.

with policing each other rather than coming together and demanding solutions to systemic problems that are inherent to the corporation itself.

An example of a systemic, plant-wide problem and its effect on the teams and the workforce is staffing levels. In other GM plants, if a given shift is short of workers, then workers are borrowed from other shifts or locations in the plant or the line might even be slowed down. The Tarrytown transplant describes the difference in stark terms:

> In Saturn, if you were to get injured and be on restriction and couldn't perform your duties, the team members would say you were not pulling your fair share and you were ostracized because you got hurt, through no fault of your own. The people on the team felt that you were letting them down. You didn't have that in the old world.[45]

Work units or teams may deal with technical issues or personnel situations that arise with other workers. Accounts of teams solving production problems by themselves or coming up with product innovations on the shop floor do warm the hearts of those who value "Yankee ingenuity." Whether workers are compensated properly for the unconditional transfer of production knowledge to the corporation remains an unanswered question. In the name of continuous improvement, workers are expected to contribute in these ways as a matter of course. Personnel issues such as vacation schedules, absenteeism, lateness, and workplace injuries also fall within the purview of a work unit. On the surface, it seems much better to try to solve production and personnel problems within one's team rather than through shopfloor disciplinarians — foremen or other management figures.[46] Yet when workers do not devise the rules but are responsible for their enforcement, workers then become divided between those who administer the rules and those who must endure the decisions.

As one former work unit counselor noted, the setup at Saturn is a "gift from heaven" from a management point of view.

> In the "old world"... if you [assembly-line worker] had a beef, it most likely ended up in a face-to-face, finger-pointing "discussion" with the foreman. Then the union would be called and the

---

45. Ibid.
46. Nelson Lichtenstein, "'The Man in the Middle': A Social History of Automobile Industry Foremen," in *On the Line: Essays in the History of Auto Work*, ed. Nelson Lichtenstein and Stephen Meyer (Urbana: University of Illinois Press, 1989), 153–89.

foreman would have to replace you on the line to talk with your representative — another beef for him or her. Then most likely the union and the foreman had the same face-to-face, finger pointing discussion. If nothing was satisfied, then the union pulled out the grievance pad and a written complaint was made. In other words, in was a real headache to deal with labor in the fair way that was expected.[47]

This approach has advantages. From a union perspective, the accumulation of grievances becomes a way to bargain effectively with management. At contract time, grievances could be dropped to gain concessions from management. In the Saturn system, a unionized work unit counselor is the person to whom one complains. The radically scaled back character of the "contract" at Saturn narrows the range of options.

There are no grievance pads at Saturn. There is no contract to point to line number, paragraph number, and say that management is violating. The contract says that it is a broad guideline. . . . A person can get fired in one module for doing the same thing another person had done in another [module who received] little if any discipline.[48]

As this former six-year veteran of work unit counselor experience noted, one can give ten different people a few paragraphs of the Memorandum of Agreement and ask them to interpret it. "Ask them how they interpreted the paragraphs they have just read. I am willing to bet you get ten different responses. Such is our 'contract.'"[49]

The difficulties that the partnership has caused at the union leadership level and between workers on the work teams comprise two levels of a multidimensional problem. Individual workers must also contend with their own internal process, their own mindset within the Saturn system. The reference earlier to "Awareness" or the "Saturnization" process hints at larger concerns that some Saturn worker have been able to identify. The Tarrytown worker noted that "management has their own agenda already, and you are made to feel that you have some input when in actuality they are just leading you to their decision. A lot of it looks good on

---

47. Former twenty-four-year GM employee, name withheld to preserve anonymity, interview by author, e-mail communication, January 11, 2002.
48. Ibid.
49. Ibid.

paper, but the reality isn't there."[50] The former Framingham GM worker was unequivocal about the matter. "It's a whole lot like GM. They just came up with a different way to brainwash the people to do what they wanted them to do and convince them they had a lot more involvement than what they had in reality."[51] When pressed on the word "brainwash," he repeated the point and then launched into a rather vivid account of the ways things used to be done in the "old world." "I don't want to say manipulating, but in the old world, they didn't brainwash. You got hired in, you were a line worker, you had a supervisor, a foreman, a general foreman, superintendent, and if you didn't do it the way the supervisor said, then your butt was kicked out the door."[52]

It would be tempting to argue that the team concept at Saturn is part of a "master plan" devised by clever management types to manipulate workers into divisions against each other. Yet the history of the inception of Saturn indicates that there was much resistance in the General Motors power structure to the delegation of power to the union. The power of visionaries within GM and the fact that GM had its back to the wall forced its hand to try anything that would, at least, halt the loss of market share to Japanese manufacturers. One does not need a conspiracy story of management scheming. The mere fact that management shares subsidiary powers while it retains the most important levers of power is enough to produce the division described above.

Power and the Partnership: The Effects on the Union

Supporters of Saturn argue that the experiences of workers should not be interpreted as a reason to reject the experiment, because *there is no alternative* but an unworkable adversarialism. For instance, Saul Rubinstein and Thomas Kochan, the authors of *Learning from Saturn: Possibilities for Corporate Governance and Employee Relations*, note rightly that adverse workers' experiences arise from the inability of the union to find a balance between representing individual interests and the need to co-manage the Saturn plant.[53] Yet their conclusion that the search for the

---

50. Former GM worker, Tarrytown, New York, interview by author, tape recording, Spring Hill, Tennessee, August 12, 2000.

51. Former Framingham employee, name withheld to preserve anonymity, interview by author, tape recording, Spring Hill, Tennessee, August 10, 2000.

52. Ibid.

53. For additional perspectives on Saturn, see Paul Osterman, Thomas A. Kochan, Richard M. Locke, and Michael J. Piore, *Working in America: A Blueprint for the New*

balance should continue is a faulty one. Instead this search needs to stop because it is impossible for the union to work out an acceptable balance in a plant that it does not own and could never hope to control. In any event, just because a manufacturing plant rejects a partnership does not mean that it is irremediably adversarial. The Tarrytown worker recalled experiences in other GM plants and made this argument:

> We were under the International Agreement and we had a basic team concept, not like at Saturn, but we got along great, we didn't have an adversarial relationship. Everything that you read at Saturn says that unless you have cooperation, then it must be adversarial. Not all plants had an adversarial relationship. You can get along with management and still have union and management, not partnered. We'd solve quality problems with management, we had an excellent union, we had the lowest absentee rate, we got along, so it doesn't necessarily have to be an adversarial relation. Saturn has the opinion that unless you are partners, the union and management are going to disagree. That's not true. Your union identity is going to get lost.[54]

An important issue is that of union democracy, which cannot be abstracted from the conditions created in a plant that features co-management. At Saturn, the estrangement of workers from each other undermines the trust that is necessary for a robust and democratic union. Unions have always had to contend with those who test the limits of solidarity. This temptation is enhanced when the very structure of the workplace is premised on the perception but not the reality of shared interests.

At Saturn, as anywhere, to gain power is both invigorating and enticing. A little power entices one into thinking more is possible. This is not a bad situation in itself. The problem is when an organization, such as a union and its leadership, ignores or denies the institutional limits of a given arrangement and forgets the people to whom it is truly accountable. As observed above, individual workers may also forget the limits of their individual situation and identify with management goals

Labor Market (Cambridge, Mass.: MIT Press, 2001), 84–86, and Seymour Melman, *After Capitalism: From Managerialism to Workplace Democracy* (New York: Alfred A. Knopf, 2001), 283–84, 288, 308–15.

54. Former GM worker, Tarrytown, New York, interview by author, tape recording, Spring Hill, Tennessee, August 12, 2000.

rather than the people with whom they work every day. When the power that one seeks is derived power or power gained from another source, the temptation to identify with the source of this power is quite powerful. This is the major problem with the Saturn and UAW partnership. The power of Local 1853 is derived from its institutional arrangement with Saturn, its partner. The premise of this union from the outset was always this partnership and the Memorandum of Agreement and the Guiding Principles that define this relationship. Local 1853 has never had the chance to develop a sense of itself as a union whose power is derived from the workers. The active engagement of workers who, in democratic solidarity, identify the issues important to them and strive to resolve them are the prerequisites for such a union. Important steps toward the necessary independence for Local 1853 occurred in a series of votes in 1999, when the partnership at Saturn came under heavy fire from the workers. But rather than rallying specifically against management, the workers looked inward and began a major housecleaning within the leadership of their union local. In February of that year, the Vision Team, the union caucus that had championed the partnership with GM ever since the beginning of Saturn, was defeated by a two-to-one margin. This meant the toppling of Mike Bennett, the head of Local 1853, and the person who was at the center of the UAW's historic agreement with GM from the beginning. The leadership currently in place is called the Movement for a Democratic Union. The fact that this election and change of leadership occurred might be viewed as an example of union democracy that its supporters so fervently wish to see at Saturn. Yet the fact that both caucuses support, in a fundamental way, the partnership between the union local and Saturn could indicate that democracy in the form of distinct choices just does not exist there.

Conclusion

Raised expectations about Saturn have eroded over the years. Workers are now left with unrealized ideals and the inability to restore even the small amount of power they once had over the conditions of production. As one worker put it, after the excitement of building a concept died down, people had to get back to the tiring reality of building cars day in and day out. In addition, many workers reported that GM is creeping back into Saturn; the line dividing GM from its subsidiary is not so clearly defined anymore. In fact, one worker called it the bastardization of Saturn — using Saturn's good name to cover the faulty ways of GM. Many are concerned about this.

Saturn raises the stakes for itself by articulating and emphasizing a specific moral outlook. In most other workplaces, the moral agenda is implicit rather than talked about and advertised. Yet what happens when moral norms, however one wishes to characterize them, go through the prism of one of the largest multinational corporations in the world? Can one still speak meaningfully about norms? Despite all the talk of teamwork and cooperation, the final decisions about the fate of Saturn do not rest with the workers or the union but with General Motors. Saturn is not a worker-owned and worker-managed cooperative; it is a capitalist corporation, and this very fact places severe limitations on the scope of the performance of its ideals, no matter how vociferously they are stated.

At the same time, despite the limits, workers still want a share in the process; they wish to be participants in determining the conditions of their work. Yet the vehicle for trying to expand upon and extend the Saturn ethic and Saturn morality is not with the corporation itself. The route is much less direct than individuals going on their own to management. The union local itself, Local 1853, becomes the precondition for the quality work life that Saturn as a whole espouses. If the union, as an autonomous and independent agent, acts in ways that are solely devoted to enhancing the power of its own members, then the conditions for trust and respect and teamwork are better approximated. Since trust and respect were the values that many Saturn workers claimed were least honored, the task for strengthening the self-identity of the union at Saturn is clear.

Three

CONFLICT AND CONTRACT IN COVENANTAL ETHICS

The working class and the employing class have nothing in common. There can be no peace so long as hunger and want are found among millions of the working people, and the few, who make up the employing class, have all the good things in life. Between these two classes a struggle must go on until the workers of the world organize as a class, take possession of the means of production, abolish the wage system, and live in harmony with the earth.

— Preamble to the Constitution of the Industrial Workers of the World

The history of labor and management relations raises the point whether contracts are the best way to structure interactions between these two parties. In the automobile industry, contracts that may appear to outsiders as the result of patient, methodical negotiation are not automatic, but founded on years of struggle.[1] Would workers be better off at workplaces shepherded by the mutual understanding that covenants are said to promote rather than the contractual model that supposedly fosters adversarial relations? Such a question assumes a distinction between contracts and covenants. It also highlights conflict as a way to assess the merits of covenants and contracts. To explore the relationship between covenant and conflict, it is necessary first to look at the way different theologians and ethicists have handled the distinction. Also, some brief points on biblical interpretation need to be raised to qualify covenantalists' appeals to the Bible as a support for their claims. A section on the different ways that covenant has been applied to the workplace will follow. This part will introduce two covenantal ethicists, Joseph Allen

---

1. See Sol Dollinger and Genora Johnson Dollinger, *Not Automatic: Women and the Left in the Forging of the Auto Workers' Union* (New York: Monthly Review Press, 2000).

and Stewart Herman, who speak specifically about conflict within their covenantal ethic. An assessment of their outlook on the relationship between conflict and covenant will help determine whether covenantal ethics is a resource for laborers.

Contracts vs. Covenants

Most proponents of covenantal ethics and theology make a sharp distinction between covenants and contracts on the basis of their theological and ethical merits. In general, contracts are viewed as agreements between parties who hold themselves and each other accountable to specific tasks or exchanges. The relationship is grounded on the performance or nonperformance of such tasks or exchanges. The contract is the mechanism that joins the contracting parties. After the contract is complete, the parties go their separate ways. Covenants are agreements or arrangements between parties that are intended to be of mutual benefit and conducive to deeper relationships between the convenanting parties. The accent is not on exact record keeping or immediate sanction for nonperformance of agreements as in contracts. Covenants recognize the already existing relationships between the parties and work to reinforce these relationships. Even more commitment between the covenanting parties is expected for the future.

While a theological and ethical distinction is made between contracts and covenants, covenantalists do acknowledge their broad linguistic and historical connections. As Max Stackhouse notes, the English language relies on a number of linguistic traditions as it pertains to covenants. The meaning of covenant includes contracts. Sacred promise, oath, bond, troth, and bounden duty are other possibilities.[2] Stewart Herman argues for the similarity of covenants and contracts since actors in both arrangements rely on "self-binding" or the agreement to submit to sanctions if one fails "to perform the specified stipulations." He notes that there are similarities between covenants in the Bible and contracts between union and management.[3]

In the context of marriage, covenant and contract are both relevant phenomena. Though most people have no idea what "covenant"

---

2. Max L. Stackhouse, *Covenant and Commitments: Faith, Family, and Economic Life* (Louisville: Westminster John Knox Press, 1997), 143.

3. Stewart W. Herman, *Durable Goods: A Covenantal Ethic for Management and Employees* (Notre Dame, Ind.: University of Notre Dame Press, 1997), 120.

means, there is some awareness that marriage should include mutual accountability, sustained commitments, and sharing without score keeping. Thus, not all couples have a positive view of prenuptial agreements because they imply distrust and the assumption that the relationship is impermanent. Still, whether a couple has such an agreement, marriage is also viewed as a contractual, legal arrangement within a covenantal context.[4]

The sharp distinction between covenant and contract has influential forebears in the United States. H. Richard Niebuhr argues in "The Idea of Covenant and American Democracy" that "covenant" has political ramifications as well as theological and ethical ones. A main point of his argument is that the ideas of covenant or federal society guided the founders at the time of the formation of American democracy. Covenant was a "fundamental pattern," according to Niebuhr, from the seventeenth to the nineteenth centuries, which was present in psychology, sociology, metaphysics, ethics, politics, and religion. A covenantal political ordering displaced a contractual order based solely on common interest. Instead of limited commitments and loyalties and the search for mutual advantage, those guided by a covenantal orientation viewed their activities as the "moral act of taking upon oneself, through promise, the responsibilities of a citizenship that bound itself in the very act of exercising its freedom. For in this covenant conception the essence of freedom does not lie in the liberty of choice among goods, but in the ability to commit oneself for the future to a cause."[5] Though Niebuhr overstates his claim that covenant broadly informed the founders of the United States (given the racist and exclusionary character of the Constitution), the sharp contrast that he made between contracts and covenants has been influential.

Another pattern in discussions of covenant and contract is to note a passing similarity while seeking to put distance between the ideas. This is characteristic of William May's formulation in *The Physician's Covenant*. He grants that, materially considered, they are "first cousins" because they involve an exchange and agreement between parties. In spirit, how-

---

4. For a theological analysis of Western marriage law that also sheds historical light on this question, see John Witte Jr., *From Sacrament to Contract: Marriage, Religion, and Law in the Western Tradition* (Louisville: Westminster John Knox Press, 1997). Also see Stackhouse, *Covenants and Commitments*, 166, notes 28 and 32.

5. H. Richard Niebuhr, "The Idea of Covenant and American Democracy," *Church History* 23 (1954): 133.

ever, they are quite different. Covenants involve a deeper dimension of people than do contracts. Contracts are insufficiently communal and the appeal to self-interest is limiting. Yet in a physician and patient relationship, there are some advantages to a contract, according to May. Informed consent, respect for the dignity of a patient, and the specification of rights, duties, conditions, and qualifications are all possible with contracts. A symmetrical and mutual relationship between the doctor and a patient is established. The patient's self-interest and the capacity to carry out his or her wishes are not only recognized but protected by law. Yet a covenantal relationship is still a better option in a medical setting, according to May. Professional obligations can tend toward a "self-interested minimalism" or a "quid pro quo" that suppresses the aspect of "gift" in human relations.[6] Contracts attend only to what is required and not necessarily to what is just. The minimalism of contracts can induce in a professional an attitude that is "too grudging, too calculating, too lacking in spontaneity, too quickly exhausted to go the second mile with patients along the road of their distress."[7] Covenantal relationships can be transformational and not merely transactional. A healer or doctor can respond to a patient's self-perceived wants and also to her or his deeper needs.[8]

As far as the Saturn Corporation is concerned, it is a fascinating place because of the collision between contracts and covenants in its philosophy. It *is* a "different kind of car company" as it tries to cultivate a covenantal understanding of relationships while maintaining a contract that governs officially the relationship between labor and management. This is also the occasion for a different kind of work ethic. At Saturn, workers are not accountable to specific tasks on the basis of a carefully worded and highly detailed contract. Instead, the goal is for workers to be so motivated by the Saturn values that they will do what is expected and required on their own without heavy-handed external coercion or

---

6. William F. May, *The Physician's Covenant: Images of the Healer in Medical Ethics*, 2d ed. (Louisville: Westminster John Knox Press, 2000), 126.

7. Ibid., 130–31.

8. The issue of clergy misconduct is another occasion to consider the relationship of contracts and covenants. David G. Bromley and Clinton H. Cress rely on a distinction of contracts from covenants to explain the nature of this violation. See David G. Bromley and Clinton H. Cress, "Narratives of Sexual Danger: A Comparative Perspective on the Emergence of the Clergy Sexual Violation Standard," in *Bad Pastors: Clergy Misconduct in Modern America*, ed. Anson Shupe, William A. Stacey, and Susan E. Darnell (New York: New York University Press, 2000), 39–68.

force. The foreman will no longer be on the line exerting managerial authority. Instead, the foreman is to be "within" each worker silently urging him or her forward to greater efficiency and productivity.

The Bible and Covenant

The theme of covenant in the Bible has been the source for the development of covenantal ethics and theology. A review of opinions on the concept of covenant in the Bible helps to evaluate the claims of covenantalists who rely on the authority of the Bible to support the significance of covenant for our own time.

The theme of covenant is a leading option for interpreters who contend that the Bible can be characterized by a main theme or metaphor. A count of the number of times that "covenant" appears in the Bible is one level on which to note the importance of this theme. "Covenant," or the Hebrew *berith*, appears in the Old Testament 286 times.[9] Another way to assess the significance of "covenant" for the Bible is etymological in character. The term "testament" in the designations Old Testament and New Testament is actually a translation for the Greek word *diatheke*. *Diatheke* (also, last will) is the term that the Septuagint (the Greek-language translation of the Old Testament) uses for the Hebrew word for covenant — *berith*. Later writers of the books of the New Testament used the Greek word *diatheke* for covenant just as the earlier translators did in composing the Septuagint.[10] These etymological connections suggest that if the very names of the major sections of the Christian Bible include the word "covenant," then the Bible must be heavily indebted to a covenantal orientation. This viewpoint has much support. Statements of this position include the following: "Covenant as idea and practical device is central to the whole of biblical literature. As idea, it sets forth the terms of a particularly biblical approach to the world. The entire worldview of the Bible and consequently the essential outlook of all biblically rooted traditions is built around the covenant idea."[11] Or, covenant is "the concept in which Israelite thought gave

---

9. Klaus Baltzer, *The Covenant Formulary: In Old Testament, Jewish, and Early Christian Writings*, trans. David E. Green (Philadelphia: Fortress Press, 1971), 6. Baltzer relies on Ludwig Koehler's count in *Lexicon in Veteris Testamenti Libros* (Leiden: Brill, 1953), 150b.

10. Steven L. McKenzie, *Covenant* (St. Louis: Chalice Press, 2000), 3.

11. Daniel J. Elazar, *Covenant and Polity in Biblical Israel: Biblical Foundations and Jewish Expressions*, vol. 1 of *Covenant Tradition in Politics* (New Brunswick, N.J.: Transaction Publishers, 1995), 64.

definitive expression to the binding of the people to God and by means of which they established firmly from the start the particularity of their knowledge of him."[12]

The viewpoint that "covenant" is the guiding perspective of the Bible needs a cautionary note. Does "covenant" always designate the same phenomenon every time it is used in the Old Testament or even in the New Testament? At a surface level, it is clear that this is not the case. A standard lexicon of ancient Hebrew notes that *berith* has two categories: covenants between God and humans, and covenants that are forged only among humans.[13] Even proponents of the importance of covenant in the Bible are cautious. For instance, George Mendenhall insists that different historical periods yield considerable variation in its definition and application. He grants that "covenant" in the Bible is *the* major metaphor used to describe the relation between God and Israel, the people of God. A covenant is "an agreement enacted between two parties in which one or both make promises under oath to perform or refrain from certain actions stipulated in advance."[14] Nonetheless, Mendenhall offers this caveat:

> In the millennium during which ancient Israelite society and thought developed and changed, and in which the biblical documents were written, the same single term — *berit* — came to be used to refer to many different types of oath-bound promises and relationships. Therefore, any study of covenant in the Bible must be sensitive to the varying social and ideological contexts associated with different types of oath-taking, and it must also be prepared to make careful distinctions between different phenomena underlying the singular use of the Hebrew word *berit*.[15]

These phenomena include treaties, loyalty oaths, and charters. In addition to the many ways that *berit* appears, there is a another consideration for Mendenhall. Covenants can be viewed either as historical events that functioned to bring about changes in behavior or as "formal

12. Walther Eichrodt, *Theology of the Old Testament*, trans. J. A. Baker (Philadelphia: Westminster Press, 1961), 1:36.

13. This is McKenzie's observation, *Covenant*, 4. The lexicon is Francis Brown, S. R. Driver, and Charles A. Briggs, *A Hebrew and English Lexicon of the Old Testament* (Oxford: Clarendon Press, 1974), 136–37.

14. George E. Mendenhall, "Covenant," *The Anchor Bible Dictionary*, ed. David Noel Freedman (New York: Doubleday, 1992), 1:1179.

15. Ibid.

or symbolic dogmatic concepts" that are matters of traditions and belief. He acknowledges the importance of "covenant" as a biblical metaphor but criticizes theologians who reduce "covenant" to an "idea" or an article of faith that does not account for covenants as "enacted realities" or historical practices.[16] Norman Gottwald expands on this insight by stressing that covenant is also rooted in social and political practices. He emphasizes this outlook to counter "later Jewish and Christian obsessions with covenant and law, under whose spell we are still inclined to read all parts of the Hebrew Bible."[17]

The covenants with Noah, Abraham, and David and with Israel at Mount Sinai have common characteristics that shape how these covenants are applied in the current day. One characteristic is God's activity as a covenant initiator. These covenants are not between equals but between one who is superior and one who is subordinate. God is depicted as one who issues commands and demands obedience. Other commentators urge nonetheless that God, despite this asymmetry of power, does not use power without restraint. Daniel Elazar notes that when God covenants with human beings, "God does not exercise His omnipotence in the affairs of men." God limits this omnipotence and "withdraws somewhat from interfering with them to give them space to be independently human. He grants humans a degree of freedom under the terms of the covenant, retaining only the authority to reward or punish the consequences of that freedom at some future date."[18] One way to read these texts is to view the inequality between the covenant-making parties as a reason for initiating the relationship. In each instance, God grants to the recipient what the recipient could not secure for himself. In the case of Noah, God granted him the time to build an ark to insure survival from the flood. For Abraham, God promised him numberless descendents even though Sarah, his wife, could not even have one child. When David was at war with his neighbors in an ongoing but uncertain bid for military supremacy, God guaranteed David and his house an everlasting kingdom.

The accounts of God's covenanting activity may be read as literal descriptions of God's actions in human lives in specifiable historical periods. Or they may be read as *interpretations* of encounters between the

---

16. Ibid., 1201.
17. Norman K. Gottwald, *The Hebrew Bible: A Socio-Literary Introduction* (Philadelphia: Fortress Press, 1985), 204.
18. Elazar, *Covenant and Polity in Biblical Israel*, 68.

human and the divine. Either way, theologians view covenanting activity as the plane on which relationships are forged between God and the people of God. Those who do not read these texts in a literal manner tend to be more open to the historical complexities that raise doubts about their meaning and intent. For them, the author(s), date(s), or place(s) of any given writing are not settled matters. Questions about the original dates and sources of covenants are matters of complex debate about the proper way to interpret and utilize ancient texts. But even with the vast historical uncertainty about the biblical narratives that describe covenants, covenantal ethicists and theologians insist on their authority to the current day.

The Managerial Love Ethic

Many discussions about covenant center on the role of management in implementing the covenantal dimension in the workplace. Since management is assumed to bear responsibility for workplace conditions, they are the ones who can control the quality of relationships on the shop floor. One manifestation of the covenantal perspective is the application of the "love ethic" to business relationships. The Protestant evangelical authors of *Business through the Eyes of Faith* urge that "love" be adopted as a style of management in which one is to be a "servant leader."[19] Such a leader does not flaunt power. "Instead our power as managers can be contained in love. Love is what is needed to enhance, build up, mature, and strengthen the cared-for person."[20] The authors complain that the larger Christian community spends too little time considering "How do I love my neighbor in business?" Another way to show love and do justice in the workplace is to enhance human dignity by creating opportunities for workers to participate in problem solving. Workers need to be assured that their ideas and creativity are wanted. "Christian managers" must foster work environments where the creation and utilization of constructive ideas can enhance the workers and thus bring "enormous benefits" to everyone.

---

19. Richard C. Chewning, John W. Eby, and Shirley J. Roels, *Business through the Eyes of Faith* (San Francisco: Harper & Row, 1990). The managerial orientation of Roels's work is evident in her essay "Organization Man, Organization Woman: Faith, Gender, and Management," in *Organization Man, Organization Woman: Calling, Leadership, and Culture* (Nashville: Abingdon Press, 1997), 17–79, especially 45–51.

20. Chewning, Eby, and Roels, *Business through the Eyes of Faith*, 93.

A similar perspective to the love ethic is Laura Nash's proposal in her book *Good Intentions Aside: A Manager's Guide to Resolving Ethical Problems.* Her argument for a covenantal business ethic draws upon no-tions of "caring" or "workings of the heart" that include and go beyond questions of legal obligation, weighing of rights, and cost-benefit calcu-lations. A covenantal ethic promises a communal morality and it places "the energy and intrinsic worth of individuals above the mechanics of an organizational system and its preordained financial strategy."[21] It is an ethic of mutual benefit that is neither explicitly self-interested nor purely other-interested.

In *Just Business: Christian Ethics for the Marketplace,* Alexander Hill also touts the virtues of "covenantal management." Similar to the au-thors above, he argues that the Christian perspective on the relationship between managers and subordinates is much broader than its legal and economic aspects. Rather, covenantal management calls on "employ-ers to demonstrate *holiness* through purity, mutual accountability and humility; *justice* through rewarding merit, compensating for harm done, recognizing substantive rights and honoring procedural rights; and *love* through empathy, mercy and sacrifice."[22] Dignity, reciprocity, servant leadership, and gift recognition are the four components of covenantal management. Christian managers are responsible for identifying and de-veloping their subordinates' gifts and talents since the skills of one's workers are of divine origin. Such acuity on the part of Christian managers is also necessary because, as Hill unabashedly declares, with the "current corporate trend toward flattening organizations, executives must find creative ways to expand their human resource base without adding new hires."[23] Covenantal managers should focus on relationships and dignity and not bottom-line efficiencies. Workers are not pieces of expendable machinery. Japanese manufacturers and the total quality movement have demonstrated that all employees, even the "low-level" ones, can make important contributions to "improving products, pro-

21. Laura L. Nash, *Good Intentions Aside: A Manager's Guide to Resolving Ethical Problems* (Boston: Harvard Business School Press, 1990), 21. Nash has followers among Christian business ethicists. See James M. Childs Jr., *Ethics in Business: Faith at Work* (Minneapolis: Fortress Press, 1995), particularly the section entitled "A Covenantal Model for Business Ethics," 66–70.

22. Alexander Hill, *Just Business: Christian Ethics for the Marketplace* (Downers Grove, Ill.: InterVarsity Press, 1997), 156.

23. Ibid., 160.

cesses and services."[24] Hill sees a direct relationship between covenantal management and teams in the workplace.

For all of the authors mentioned above, the Herman Miller Company is an exemplar of covenantalism in the workplace. Max De Pree, the chief executive officer of Herman Miller and the son of the founder, articulates a philosophy of corporate leadership that appeals directly to the value of covenants at work. In *Leadership Is an Art,* he argues that leaders "owe a covenant" to their corporation or institution. Covenants "bind people together," and the people who compose the company or nonprofit are enabled by a covenant to "meet their corporate needs by meeting the needs of one another."[25]

De Pree's philosophy of corporate management is participatory. All employees have the "right" and the "duty" to influence decision making. Decisions are not to be arbitrary, secret, or removed from questioning. Importantly, he notes that participatory management it is not democratic. One may have a say but not a vote. Participation and covenant are directly related. The forging of covenantal relationships makes participation in the organization possible. Since such relations involve trust and a degree of vulnerability, people from diverse sectors of the organization are inclined to take risks and get involved. When this happens, deep needs can be met and work can have meaning and fulfillment.

Contracts, on the other hand, break down when conflict breaks out. They do not allow people to reach their potential. They express only a small part of relationships. Contracts have enabled capitalism to emerge, but capitalism has been too exclusive and too sparing when sharing the results. While De Pree does "not know of a better system," capitalism can be improved if it adopts covenantal relationships and thus is more inclusive. In this way, unusual people are accepted and unusual ideas are considered; risk is tolerated and errors are forgiven. In sum, De Pree is "convinced that the best management process for today's environment is participative management based on covenantal relationships."[26] His goal for Herman Miller is for the company to be viewed not as a corporation but as a "group of people working intimately within a covenantal relationship" such that people will say, "Those folks are a gift to the spirit."[27]

---

24. Ibid.
25. Max De Pree, *Leadership Is an Art* (New York: Bantam Doubleday Dell, 1989), 15.
26. Ibid., 61.
27. Ibid., 62.

Covenants and the Workplace in Public Theology

A much more expansive view of covenants is found in the work of Max
Stackhouse, who connects covenants with public theology, that is, a
theology that is unmistakably Christian but also able to address a wider,
even non-Christian audience on matters of public or general concern.
He considers covenant an indispensable theme for a public theology because it supplies the necessary precondition for a public to exist at all. A
true public is a community of people who are accountable to each other.
This claim is grounded in an interpretation of the biblical tradition that
considers covenant as a gift from God who "bonds the human will to
God's justice and to the neighbor in structures of mutual accountability."[28] The structures of authority that are constitutive of covenant are
based on a higher law made up of the terms and limits that God sets for
our lives together. Known as "natural law," it is universally valid and can
be apprehended, in part, through human reason without the need for
God's explicit revelation through "special" or direct revelation. "A common plumb line stands beyond all cultures, beyond all particular codes
of civil laws and institutionalized rules. These laws are ethically valid
whether or not they are observed in particular societies."[29] Humans are
created beings within a created world of "objective mandates" that include fidelity, obedience, and love, to which we are accountable despite
the fact they are not of human construction.[30] Leaders among us are to
"regard, serve, and care for those in lower positions."[31]

The uncertainty that surrounds the use of biblical materials to pin
down the origin and meaning of covenant is not an argument to dis-
count that phenomenon, according to Stackhouse. The biblical writers
applied a term that was already available to them to describe their relationship to God. The possibility that covenants have "primitive cultic"
origins is not a reason to dismiss them. Rather, it vindicates the view
that covenants are part of the created order. Biblical writers recognized
the wisdom of such activity in their own time and applied the term to
characterize their understanding of the "relationship of God to chosen
persons." At the core of such relationships is "an ordered liberty that

---

28. Max L. Stackhouse, *Public Theology and Political Economy: Christian Stewardship in
Modern Society* (Grand Rapids, Mich.: Wm. B. Eerdmans Publishing Co. for Commission
on Stewardship, National Council of the Churches of Christ in the U.S.A., 1987), 26.
29. Ibid., 28.
30. Ibid., 27.
31. Ibid.

interwove righteousness and power, law and promise, and thus a form of structured accountability that allowed all people to deal justly with one another and to manage scarce resources and competing loyalties with the greatest possible harmony."[32]

The bridge between the theological and the ethical perspectives on covenant is stated very clearly by Stackhouse. Each manifestation of covenant whether it entails relationships such as "friend-friend, husband-wife, parent-child, tribe-tribe, king-people, kingdom-kingdom, employer-employee, teacher-disciple, judge-accused, redeemer-humanity" represents "an ethical outworking" of the divine-human relationship.[33] There is much at stake in a covenantal perspective. Without it, one is left with the feudalism of patriarchy or the arbitrary relativism of contractualism.[34] Contractualism assumes that there are neither objective nor absolute moral guidelines for human relations and that all religions, theologies, and ethics are formed only by acts of the will and imagination.[35] Stackhouse describes this situation as "contractual egoism." Such egoism is a reduction to the individual for whom the satisfaction of needs is sovereign.[36] One's only recourse is an "understanding of and a commitment to covenantal mutuality under God." In this way, moral and spiritual coherence can be experienced instead of a "seething, chaotic mass of dominations and arbitrariness."[37]

One example of Stackhouse's covenantal orientation applied to the workplace includes the assertions found in "A Postcommunist Manifesto: Public Theology after the Collapse of Socialism." Stackhouse and co-author Dennis McCann attempt to situate themselves between socialism and libertarian neoconservatism. Socialism is "more exploitative" and it impoverishes people. Modern capitalism, despite its flaws, engenders greater cooperation. People must embrace a version of capitalism that "uses law, politics, education and especially theology and ethics to constrain the temptations to exploitation and greed everywhere."[38] A

32. Stackhouse, *Covenant and Commitments*, 142.
33. Ibid., 142.
34. Stackhouse, *Public Theology and Political Economy*, 27.
35. Ibid., 26–27.
36. Stackhouse, *Covenant and Commitments*, 155.
37. Ibid.
38. Max L. Stackhouse and Dennis P. McCann, "A Postcommunist Manifesto: Public Theology after the Collapse of Socialism," in *On Moral Business: Classical and Contemporary Resources for Ethics in Economic Life*, ed. Max L. Stackhouse, Dennis P. McCann, Shirley J. Roels, Preston N. Williams (Grand Rapids, Mich.: William B. Eerdmans, 1995), 950.

public theology must be adequate to the task of providing "theological help" to the challenge of the new economy. This help comes in the form of a "covenant for corporations," which is the recognition that corporations have become "the social form distinctive of every cooperative human activity outside the family, the government and personal friendships."[39] Modern business corporations could become a "worldly ecclesia" in a way equal to hospitals, unions, parties, schools, voluntary organizations, and cultural institutions.[40] For corporations to fulfill their calling as a "secular form of covenantal community," Christian leaders must help business people build organizations that are associations of "interdependent people seeking to produce goods and services that benefit the commonwealth" as opposed to organizations that seek maximum immediate advantage.[41] If a public theology could help people overcome their contempt for corporations as "mere money machines," then "we can even learn to love them as we have learned to love our churches, neighborhoods, nations, schools and hospitals."[42] In a postsocialist world, Stackhouse and McCann affirm that such a view of the corporation is a theological topic worthy of the work of public theologians.[43]

A Critique of the Managerial Love Ethic

The fledgling field of covenantal business ethics has not yet found a way to consider the experience of workers who must live out the actual consequences of a covenantal business ethic. This deficiency has been mitigated somewhat with the publication of Stewart Herman's book entitled *Durable Goods: A Covenantal Ethic for Management and Employees* (1997). His book is an important contribution to Protestant business ethics because of his attempt to uphold the ethical and practical viability of a covenantal ethic while recognizing that workers have interests that diverge from those of their employers. Herman disagrees with those he labels "ethical managerialists" who assume that what is good for management is also good for workers. The perspective of workers is taken

39. Ibid., 952.

40. Ibid.

41. Ibid., 953.

42. Ibid.

43. More praise for capitalism can be found in Stackhouse's essay "Christian Social Ethics in a Global Era: Reforming Protestant Views" in *Christian Social Ethics in a Global Era* (Nashville: Abingdon Press, 1995), 11–73.

seriously in this book with his recounting of labor history and his concerns about managerial "will to power." This sets him at odds with other Protestant business ethicists who also employ the covenantal model to envision ideal business practices but rarely discuss labor history, unions, or labor-management conflict.[44]

As a self-described moderate, Herman tries to steer "a middle course" between what he calls "ethical managerialism" and the "radical critics."[45] He aspires to a "Christian realism which hews a middle way between the optimism of those ethicists who think that management alone can define and achieve genuine cooperation and moral community within firms, and the pessimism of dissenting voices who believe that management can achieve nothing of the sort."[46] This middle course requires a methodological commitment to "moral objectivity" which affirms equally the goals and interests of both management and employees. Only in this way can a vision of genuine cooperation be realized. This "relative neutrality" necessitates seeing congruent interests and also the divergent interests between employers and employees. This recognition of divergent interests is contrary to a pure ethical managerialism that sees workplace relationships as "essentially cooperative." The radical critics who see labor relations as "essentially conflictive" are also in error. Rather, a covenantal business ethic "intertwines irreducible elements of both conflict and cooperation."[47]

Herman's method is to employ a model of moral reasoning that focuses on the *actual* history of cooperation and conflict. For him, this is more important than formal argumentation about the "proper" relationship between management and employees. As such, Herman draws upon sources in labor-management relations, the social-scientific field of organization theory, and the Bible, which provides a "normative focus" for charting the strategies, tactics, and principles that God employs in dealing with God's people. This relationship is a model for covenantal relations between management and employees.

---

44. Stewart W. Herman, *Durable Goods: A Covenantal Ethic for Management and Employees* (Notre Dame, Ind.: University of Notre Dame Press, 1997), 12.

45. Herman includes David Krueger's work among the ethical managerialists. See David A. Krueger, *Keeping Faith at Work: The Christian in the Workplace* (Nashville: Abingdon Press, 1994). Another important example of Krueger's managerialist orientation is his essay "The Business Corporation and Productive Justice in the Global Economy" in *The Business Corporation and Productive Justice* (Nashville: Abingdon Press, 1997), 17–98.

46. Herman, *Durable Goods*, 4–5.

47. Ibid., 16.

The practice of forming a "covenant" arises when the actors in a relationship "encounter *durable* or *ineradicable* contingencies in each other, and seek to cope with them *by making enduring commitments.*"[48] Management and employees present any number of "contingencies" to each other that cannot be covered in full by any contract. This is not to say that contracts ought not to be formed. In fact, contracts are a form of covenanting insofar as they cause each side to bind themselves to commitments that lessen the number of contingencies that they could inflict on each other. Since contingencies (for good or for harm) are never completely eliminated, covenants help both parties embrace activities that are mutually beneficial. A covenantal bond in corporations develops when "both sides refrain from taking advantage of their power over each other: as they keep their promises despite adverse conditions; as they engage in nonobligatory concessions or spontaneous gestures of good will; as they adhere to unwritten as well as written norms of procedural justice; as they avoid manipulating and deceiving each other; and so forth."[49]

From the perspective of a covenantal business ethic, cooperation has an "intrinsic" value. Cooperation is the mode for coordinating activity to achieve a productive end. It does not mean compliance or servitude; cooperation is the antithesis of disorganization and conflict. According to Herman, cooperation is "costly" for both employers and employees because they must relinquish a degree of coercive power. Employers lose power when they delegate decision making to employees; laborers who truly desire cooperation must be open to the contingencies that employers present to them in the workplace. Laborers must give up certain forms of resistance and take a chance that management will remain cooperative and not renege on their own promises. Cooperation means that both sides must move from the "terrain of war" to the "terrain of politics." Influence tactics, not coercion, must be the mode of action in cooperative behavior. The balance between "affirmations of trustworthiness" and "bids for change" is a difficult one and can be only sustained through "ongoing gestures" that show a commitment by each party to each other.[50]

The effort to achieve cooperation in business is worthwhile for Herman because it mirrors, though distantly, "the nature of God's struggle

---

48. Ibid., 38–39.
49. Ibid., 40.
50. Ibid., 172.

with God's very human people."[51] From the perspective of a covenant, cooperation is a moral achievement because it transforms the participants who are engaged in this "mutual entrustment of contingent wills."[52] The theological principle is that "just as God chooses to accept, and then recruit, the contingent energies and will of the people for the never-ending work of building up covenantal relations, so management and employees are to enlist rather than suppress the contingent energies of each other."[53] When this occurs in the workplace, then the "common" good is realized. Individual wills become united in a common aim and a larger whole is produced. Cooperation demands so much more of employees and employers than does coercion or compliance. As such, it is inherently valuable. Though employers, in a cooperative work environment, give up power by delegating decision making to workers, they gain workers with an "awakened sense of responsibility." In this environment, both employees and management gain an "expanded vision." Intensified consultation between the parties becomes possible and ever-deepening ties of mutuality are forged. Both parties must listen to each other and acknowledge each other's interests and proposals. Since coercion is no longer an option, persuasion must be used. This means that people must listen to and acknowledge each other.

Herman acknowledges that his position of "covenantal realism" is not likely to please either ethical managerialists or radical critics "but it may appeal to realists as an effort to give the moral claims of both management and employees relatively equal weight."[54] The appeal to covenant in Christian business ethics provides a common base point to "integrate" divergent Christian ethical viewpoints in both Protestant and Catholic circles. It has normative power because of its basis in actual labor-management relations. "Covenant" has descriptive power too as there is a visible covenantal logic within the history of employment relations in the United States.

The way to know that God is working to bring about covenantal relationships between labor and management is to explore the history of labor and management relations to see what "moral parameters" have developed within it. The meaning of covenantal love and justice must be sought within human relationships, according to Herman. In this

---

51. Ibid., 176.
52. Ibid.
53. Ibid., 180.
54. Ibid., 190.

way, a normative biblical vision can be developed that respects this history. Following God's modeling of covenant-building behavior over the "long sweep of biblical narrative," each side must bind themselves and resolutely resist exploiting each other's weaknesses. Both principles of managerial prerogative and employee self-representation must recognize that employees ought to be engaged in governing the work process. This is "active cooperation" which calls on employees to internalize freedom and responsibility so that their work is consistent with the business goals of management.

Covenantal Business Ethics and Conflict

Covenantal ethicists converge on the point that a "harmonious" relationship in the workplace is the ideal for which workers and managers must strive. Conflict is the deviation to be corrected. Rarely are "peaceful" relations deemed a deep ethical problem that must be held up to unsparing scrutiny. The prospect that peace may be unjust and a bulwark to preserve inequality and exclusivity is easier to miss as an ethical issue. There are two covenantal ethicists who deserve attention in this regard, not because of any enthusiastic advocacy of conflict per se, but because of their willingness to discuss conflict and coercion as an aspect of a covenantal ethic. Stewart Herman was mentioned above and will be discussed again below. A predecessor in this regard is Joseph Allen. His book *Love and Conflict: A Covenantal Model of Christian Ethics* predates the work of many covenantal ethicists yet his insights about conflict and covenant have been neglected.

Allen's perspective is particularly significant because he supports a covenantal orientation to human relationships while accepting that conflict is an "inescapable feature of life."[55] People have conflicting moral claims, people or groups of people have interests that are in conflict, and, finally, people struggle over their competing interests. Conflict poses moral problems, but it is not evil in itself. The issue is what type of conflict is involved. His goal is to discuss the standard of love in Christian ethics, the problem of conflict, and the way our "special moral relationships" are affected by the reality of both love and conflict. He does specify conflict, in particular, as posing a moral problem. But conflict is

---

55. Joseph L. Allen, *Love and Conflict: A Covenantal Model of Christian Ethics* (Nashville: Abingdon Press, 1984), 9.

not always morally problematic. There is always an element of conflict in every relationship. Given that conflict is inescapable, what significance does it have within a covenantal framework in theological ethics?

The three arenas that Allen refers to as "special covenants" are marriage, political community, and the church. Within the context of political community he mentions, in passing, labor-management issues. He speaks of the "destructive effects of serious domestic political conflict" in many cities and towns that are divided by a "bitter labor-management dispute."[56] Thus his comments about politics and covenant are of particular interest. He is clear on his position. "Conflict is not incompatible with covenant; indeed, some kinds of conflict help people express what is implied in living faithfully with one another in the same political community."[57] Yet not all conflicts tend toward the well-being of communities.

Allen asks those who are engaged in political conflict to remember that political community is a kind of covenant, including, presumably, both labor and management. Thus, if labor and management engage in conflict, they must recognize that what binds people in God's eyes is greater than the causes of division. Mutual obligation and not party spirit must be cultivated. The parties must seek points of convergence so as not to defeat one's opponents but to "resolve this quarrel within the family"[58] and promote the common good. This involves a process of discernment of whether to intensify or minimize the level of the conflict. Since even one's adversary is still a covenant member, one should avoid casting one's opponent as an enemy who must be removed or eliminated. The activity of politics is a high calling and should be transformational so that the enhancement of community is possible.

The guidelines that Allen offers for living within political community are meant to set a limit on the justifiable instances of violence and coercion. He argues that there is a need for a general theory of justifiable violence and coercion that is covenantally compatible. Christian ethics, in the tradition of Augustine and Aquinas, has a just war tradition to adjudicate the moral claims and counterclaims applied to activities that arise in the course of engaging in war. In similar fashion, just war criteria can be applied to illuminate the ethics of "nonviolently coercive

---

56. Ibid., 276.
57. Ibid.
58. Ibid., 278.

actions." A theory of justifiable coercion that expresses covenant love must include conditions for the resort to and the means of coercion. The former include legitimate authority, justifiable cause, right intention, proportionality, reasonable chance of success, and last resort. Just as all of these must be present to constitute a just war, so they must be present for any recourse to coercion. As for the means, these include proportionality and the principle of discrimination. The point throughout is to provide for the restraint of wrongdoers when necessary. In such instances, the practice of justifiable coercion "is the answer that best expresses the meaning of covenant love."[59]

The idea that conflict is inevitable and can achieve certain moral goods falls broadly within the tradition of Reinhold Niebuhr and his insights into the nature of society. Allen is conscious of his dependence on Niebuhr while noting some important differences. For instance, the origin of conflict is not primarily sinful egoism as with Niebuhr but rather from the limitations inherent to human beings as created beings. Allen also critiques Niebuhr's elevated view of sacrificial love because it does not wholeheartedly endorse the positive goods of conflict. Niebuhr argues that good can come from conflict but at the cost of not reaching the highest norm of sacrificial love. Covenant love is less suspicious of conflict overall and, in fact, requires that one participate in the conflict of interests and social conflict when covenantal relations are threatened.

Stewart Herman's view of conflict does not have Allen's functionalist optimism that conflict can redound to the ultimate benefit of the participants. In Herman's covenantal perspective, "cooperation is much to be preferred over conflict."[60] As for coercion, a mode by which conflicts are carried out, Herman concedes that Niebuhr is correct to insist on its indispensability for achieving justice and order. Yet even when it is an effective means to hold management accountable for their past deeds or for promises of reform, it is "at best of limited usefulness for introducing a covenantal quality into management-employee relations."[61] External coercion can set off a spiral of "mutually reinforcing resistance and counterresistance" or a spiral of "tit for tat."[62] As such, it undermines the goal of covenant building among employees and management.

---

59. Ibid., 217.
60. Herman, *Durable Goods*, 59.
61. Ibid., 128.
62. Ibid., 128, 129.

According to Herman, God's larger strategy in covenants is to move "antagonistic partners towards internalizing the values of lovingkindness and justice, rather than relying upon external agencies to enforce these values."[63]

Another option is the "genius of contracts." Contracts are one way for the respective parties to engage in self- or internalized constraint. Herman deems that this is a type of coercion. In signing contracts, "both sides effectively offer themselves up as hostages to each other."[64] He cites Joseph Allen's book and agrees that contracts fall short of a full covenantal ideal because they are bargains and not offers, are of limited time value, are contingent upon the actions of the contractors, and are instrumentalist in their view of persons. In this way, Herman also holds to a distinction between contracts and covenants. But, in an all-important caveat, Herman sees that labor contracts do have an "integral" relationship with covenants because, for both, there is a "specific kind of self-binding."[65] Contracts can be the template upon which a more full-bodied set of commitments can be made to each other in the future. They can be the beginning rather than the terminus of future and deeper relations.

For Herman, it comes down to what will best promote the internalization of norms appropriate to a covenantal relationship. "Here a categorical preference can be asserted. Internalized restraint always is superior to external coercion."[66] This type of restraint or the willingness to accept sanctions for the nonperformance of contract regulations must be cultivated and nourished. Thus, employee tactics are judged by whether they "move management towards absorbing covenantal values as effective guidelines for their action."[67] Herman's judgment is that the tactics of workers from the 1930s to the 1950s that enforced the contracts were necessary and "tragic" conditions for achieving the goals of that day. Moreover, they produced a "potent and enduring counterresistance" among employers. Thus workers will need another "surge of militancy" to lift service workers and temporary workers into prosperity.

---

63. Ibid., 129.
64. Ibid.
65. Ibid., 130.
66. Ibid.
67. Ibid., 133.

Assessment of Covenantal Business Ethics

Workers across the country, blue collar and white, are facing multiple tragedies. Full-time poverty wage work, no health or life insurance, and the continuous erosion of leisure time in the spirit of "teamwork" and flexibility are some of them.[68] It is hardly "tragic" that militant workers rose up and demanded just wages and decent working conditions in the 1930s. The real tragedy would have been if they did not. Such is the situation now. Commentators such as Herman offer no way out of the time binds and the double binds of overwork and underpay when he argues that "however necessary coercive tactics may be for broader social welfare, they offer too limited a moral horizon for a covenantal ethic."[69] Perhaps the limited moral horizon is endemic to the covenantal ethic rather than the coercive actions and militancy that promote social welfare. For instance, blue-collar workers at Saturn barely have enough time to keep up with line speed to worry about whether they are, to repeat Herman's words, moving "management towards absorbing covenantal values as effective guidelines for their action."[70] The shocking idea that workers could be engaged in such activity is an example of the ways that covenantal ethicists are out of touch with workplace realities. If workers could move management to provide monetary value for the work that they do, then maybe a leisurely discussion about covenantal values could ensue.

Corporations are hardly hostages at negotiation time. The true hostages are laborers who have had to submit to corporate demands for concessions and give-backs and the undemocratic unions that have sold out their own union brothers and sisters. Even for commentators such as Herman, who tries to hew the middle ground between ethical managerialism and the "radical critics," the middle ground itself is riddled with corporate interests that are only too happy for Christian ethicists and for the church to pull back from a full assessment of the damage done to working-class interests. This was true during the Gilded Age of nineteenth-century American capitalism, and it is true today.

---

68. See Jill A. Fraser, *White-Collar Sweatshop: The Deterioration of Work and Its Rewards in Corporate America* (New York: W. W. Norton, 2001) and Barbara Ehrenreich, *Nickel and Dimed: On (Not) Getting By in America* (New York: Henry Holt, 2001).

69. Herman, *Durable Goods*, 146. See Arlie R. Hochschild, *The Time Bind: When Work Becomes Home and Home Becomes Work* (New York: Henry Holt, 2001) and Juliet B. Schor, *The Overworked American: The Unexpected Decline of Leisure* (New York: Basic Books, 1991).

70. Herman, *Durable Goods*, 133.

Contemporary Protestant Christian economic and business ethicists are apologists for managerial interests. They have quaffed freely of the formula that Margaret Thatcher prescribes: there is no alternative; the best that we can do is a better capitalism; the idea that another world is possible is inconceivable.

The emphasis on cooperation among many covenantal ethicists and the references to Japanese management techniques suggest affinities between a covenantal business ethic and the proliferation of employee participation programs since the 1970s. But covenantal ethicists are short on the details of the implementation of their covenantal norms. If they were to discuss, in any depth, the programs widely practiced in unionized and nonunionized workplaces across the country, they would find the actual practices in violation of the covenantal norms that they hold dear. The managerial bias and the lack of attention to the day-to-day conditions of the working class do not suggest that most covenantal business ethicists will have the resources to resist the deficiencies of the employee participation workplace paradigm. So far, only Stewart Herman has paid any attention to labor history. In this way, he has been able to identify the pro-business orientation of many of his colleagues. Still, his attempt to "steer the middle course" puts him in an awkward and untenable position of trying to have it both ways. He does not want to prioritize the claims of either the working class or of management. In this way, his work is reminiscent of many proponents of employee participation programs who also argue that they are trying to steer between, and fairly adjudicate, the competing claims of management and workers in the workplace. One issue is how the implementation of Herman's covenantal ethic will avoid falling into the trap that management sets for unions when it proposes to develop such programs. It is not difficult to imagine the energetic retorts of covenantal business ethicists who would claim that a careful balance, in theory and in practice, between covenanting parties is exactly opposed to a prioritization of the interests of capital. Yet such a balance is impossible in the face of the enormous power that the capitalist class currently exerts over the working class. Cooperation becomes a dangerous game that workers cannot afford to play. In an ideal world, a spirit of mutual concession would seem appropriate. Yet in the world as it is, the world in which ethics is considered and practiced, a painstaking examination of such imbalances must be the starting point of any proposal. Such work remains to be done among covenantal business ethicists.

The distinction that covenantal ethicists make between contracts and covenants is a crucial one. Contracts represent for them the current reality that has to be transcended in favor of fulfilling the ideal that covenants represent. As discussed above, the contrast between contracts and covenant is not absolute for all covenantalists. For Herman, he recognizes that contracts are a constituent dimension to covenants and represent the beginning steps for workers to realize their goals. The goal in the next chapters is not to forge a defense of contracts. Nor is it to provide a justification for the post–World War II labor-capital compact that has institutionalized labor relations and deracinated the radical and militant potential of workers in the United States. Yet in the unreflective corporatist regime in which the U.S. working class finds itself today, the mere fact of having a contract to define and protect its interests is a good first step away from the slippery slope that the proponents of flexibility advocate. The way that the postwar labor movement has suffered under the contractualist ideology of AFL-CIO leaders such as George Meany and Lane Kirkland is incalculable.[71] The solution, however, is not to move beyond contracts to a theological construct that one can only hope that corporations will adopt. The solution is certainly not the adoption and promulgation of biblical covenantal norms that rely on highly contested views of their origin and meaning. The universalization of such norms and the assumption that there is a God who continues to urge such relations upon workers is by no means a settled matter for the working class. In part, the solution is hard-nosed organizing and the unreserved militancy of workers in defense of their interests. In the words that often accompany the black cat that symbolizes the Industrial Workers of the World, "direct action gets the goods."[72]

---

71. See Paul Buhle, *Taking Care of Business: Samuel Gompers, George Meany, Lane Kirkland, and the Tragedy of American Labor* (New York: Monthly Review Press, 1999).

72. The screeching black cat is one of the symbols of the Industrial Workers of the World. Founded in 1905, the IWW, or Wobblies, advocates industrial democracy through "one big union" of all workers. Their organizing victory at the Lawrence, Massachusetts, textile strike in 1912 is one of the high points of its long history.

Four

THE CIVIL WAR BETWEEN LABOR AND CAPITAL

These early years saw the beginning of America's industrial life. Hand and hand with the growth of factories and the expansion of railroads, with the accumulation of capital and the rise of banks, came anti-labor legislation. Came strikes. Came violence. Came the belief in the hearts and minds of workers that legislatures but carry out the will of the industrialists.
— Mother Jones[1]

The struggles between labor and capital from the close of the Civil War until just after World War I were outright examples of class warfare. Desperate workers with nothing to lose went head to head with company thugs, local police, the Pinkerton Detective Agency, state militias, and federal troops. The yawning chasm between ordinary workers and the capitalists of that day was plain to every worker, every day. Yet there were occasions when the deteriorating relationships between workers and capitalists captured everyone's attention — from farmers to industrialists. Protestant social Christians stepped into the quarrel and appealed to both sides to strive toward industrial peace achieved through cooperation. Social Christians also understood cooperation as an alternative to capitalism that stressed common ownership of an enterprise. But whether they referred to cooperatives or cooperation between labor and capital, the social Christian goal was to find a way to stop the disruption of the social order. The social gospelers, as they would later be called, cannot be understood properly outside of the ferocious struggles between labor and capital. Even the cursory glimpse that this chapter provides

---

1. Mother [Mary] Jones, *The Autobiography of Mother Jones* (Chicago: Charles H. Kerr, 1972), 16.

of their work is a historical reminder that current appeals for cooperation among contemporary covenantal ethicists have a long historical lineage.

The Great Upheaval of 1877 is one of the most stunning examples of the raging gap between the interests of workers and the few for whom they worked. A look at this amazing year in American history shows that capitalism, while quite dominant, was not uncontested. Socialists, communists, and the cooperative and populist movements served notice that capital's dominance, while substantial, was not yet complete. In this current era of "capitalism triumphant," it may be difficult to recall that such a time in U.S. history ever existed.

Farm to Factory, Artisan to Worker

The transition from an agriculturally based labor force to one engaged in large-scale industry is integral to the history of the United States in the nineteenth century. Herbert Gutman remarked that relatively few Americans had "direct contact with an industrial *society*" before 1850.[2] Afterward, "rapid industrialization altered the social structure, and the process left few untouched. Depending upon circumstances, these social changes meant more or less opportunity for workers, but nearly all felt greater dependence and profoundly different patterns of work discipline."[3] The new work discipline coupled with technological advances in industrial production forever changed the nature of labor for the nations' workers. A few statistics provide a snapshot of the quantum leaps in productivity as a result of the introduction of machine technologies. Before the Bessemer process was introduced, three to five tons of steel could be produced from iron per day. Afterward, the same amount of steel could be processed in only fifteen minutes. "Before the Civil War it took 61 hours of labor to produce an acre of wheat. By 1900, it took 3 hours, 19 minutes.... In 1860, 14 million tons of coal were mined; by 1884 it was 100 million tons. More coal meant more steel, because coal

---

2. Herbert G. Gutman, "Protestantism and the American Labor Movement," in *Work, Culture, and Society in Industrializing America: Essays in American Working-Class and Social History* (New York: Vintage Books, 1977), 80.

3. Ibid. For a firsthand account of how industrial development affected the lives of farm workers, see Thomas Dublin, ed., *Farm to Factory: Women's Letters, 1830–1860*, 2d ed. (New York: Columbia University Press, 1993).

furnaces converted iron into steel; by 1880 a million tons of steel were being produced; by 1910, 25 million tons."[4]

Advances in technology and vast increases in worker productivity affected the self-understanding of American workers as "laborers." Bruce Laurie's title of his concise history of labor in the nineteenth century, *Artisans into Workers*, sums up this shift rather aptly.[5] Artisans were laborers who had an intimate knowledge of the work process coupled with considerable control over the pace and structure of the work. Laurie quotes Henry Clark Wright, a hatter, who reported: "I felt real satisfaction in being able to make a hat because I loved to contemplate the work, and because I felt pleasure in carrying through the various stages."[6] To use the words of Wright the hatter, de-skilling meant stealing the pleasure by taking away the stages. To separate the stages in any multi-step production task over many people in a rationalized, coordinated manner is only possible with highly advanced knowledge of the production process. The gradual transference of craft knowledge, or "secrets of the trade," to managers in the nineteenth century enabled them to gain control of the production process. Mass production then became possible. High-paid and independent artisans were no longer necessary and viewed as a throwback to a less efficient and less profitable time. Highly developed craft knowledge was no longer a necessary job qualification.

The transition from an artisanal sensibility to that of an unskilled worker was not uniform across the workplaces of the United States. Workers in the second and third generation of the industrial experience regarded both the division of labor and machine production as commonplace.[7] But, as David Montgomery noted, these workers still retained "a form of control of productive processes which became increasingly collective, deliberate and aggressive."[8] This control was not static but a "struggle" and a "chronic battle in industrial life."[9] Craftsmen had superior knowledge, self-direction, and even supervisory responsibilities over one or more helpers whom the craftsmen themselves had hired.

---

4. Howard Zinn, *A People's History of the United States* (New York: HarperPerennial, 1990), 247.

5. Bruce Laurie, *Artisans into Workers: Labor in Nineteenth-Century America* (New York: Hill and Wang, 1989).

6. Ibid., 36.

7. David Montgomery, *Workers' Control in America: Studies in the History of Work, Technology, and Labor Struggles* (Cambridge: Cambridge University Press, 1979), 10.

8. Ibid., 10.

9. Ibid.

A look at the iron rollers at the Columbus Iron Works in Ohio provides a glimpse into the meaning of workers' control in the iron industry in the 1870s. The "moral code" developed among the iron rollers is a form of creative resistance to workplace conditions that threatened their well-being. The first aspect of this code is called the "stint," which is the productivity quota that the workers set for themselves. Despite pressure from employers and the increased pace caused by technological improvements, workers used their knowledge of the work process to set and maintain their own production levels. Such tactics on the part of iron workers is reflective of the "craftsmen's ethical code."[10] The workers were engaged in a distinctive "work ethic" to keep production levels manageable. Then contemporary sources considered unlimited output a cause of periodic unemployment, drink, and debauchery. On the other hand, restricted output was a matter of unselfish brotherhood, personal dignity, and cultivation of the mind.[11] A worker who did the work of two workers or operated more than one machine could be expelled from the union. Such work was "dirty work." To "undermine" or "connive" another worker's job was to break the "mutualistic ethical code" among the workers.[12]

The workers' mutualistic ethical code was not shared by all theologians who were concerned about the problems with capitalism. During the time when Frederick Taylor's scientific management techniques were turning artisans into workers, Washington Gladden, the first of the social gospel proponents, had these strident words about the inefficiencies of segmented job descriptions:

> It cannot be denied that in the attempt to protect themselves against oppression the unions have made many rules and restrictions which are often extremely vexatious to all who deal with them. . . . The kind of rules which are often insisted upon, regulating the cooperation of the trades, forbidding a plasterer to drive a nail or a plumber to do the simplest task which belongs to a bricklayer, rigidly fixing the hours of labor and making it a misdemeanor for a workman to finish a job if fifteen minutes of work remain at the closing hour — all such petty restrictions are a just cause of complaint. They require men to act in outrageously dis-

---

10. Ibid., 13.
11. Ibid.
12. Ibid., 14.

obliging and unneighborly ways; they are a training in ill nature and unfriendliness.[13]

The mutualism among the workers was not the only mode of resistance. The formation of union work rules was also an important way to codify moral consciousness. While wages were increasingly negotiated with employers after 1860, work rules were sometimes set by the employees. They were not usually negotiated with the employer or codified in a contract. If an employer insisted on work that violated these rules, workers were expected to join each other and walk off the job until work demands were reversed.[14]

Another strategy of worker control involved the organization of workers, not only within a union, but across union lines. Unions engaged in sympathetic strikes and supported each other across trade lines as an expression of class solidarity. In words that twenty-first-century covenantal ethicists might find interesting, a resolution at the 1895 convention of the American Federation of Labor urged unions "not to tie themselves up with contracts so that they cannot help each other when able" but to band together to help one another. "The words union, federation implied [such activity]."[15]

Working-class struggle to control the pace and structure of labor within the workplace is only one aspect of resistance to capitalism. Strikes outside the workplace, authorized or not, supported the efforts of resistance within. When workers caught that spirit and took their concerns to the streets and spread discontent from town to town and city to city, they made history in a new way. Such is the significance of 1877. There were moments that year when the working class not only achieved some measure of justice in the workplace, but achieved direct political power that thoroughly frightened state and federal authorities. Though the Civil War was over, a new civil war between labor and capital broke out. The intensity of the conflict suggests the immense power and money at stake. The fruits of the workers' toil were buried in the strong coffers of a few. Workers across the country in 1877 were determined to get it out.

---

13. Washington Gladden, *The Labor Question* (Boston: Pilgrim Press, 1911), 10–13.
14. Montgomery, *Workers' Control in America*, 16.
15. Ibid., 23.

The Panic of 1873 and the Great Strikes of 1877

The Panic of 1873 that toppled the top banking house in the United States, Jay Cooke and Company, rippled throughout the country in a severe economic depression. The stock market closed down in September and by the end of December, nearly fifty-two hundred businesses worth over $200 million shut their doors. One million industrial workers were unemployed. Other workers went on strike because of wage cuts that exceeded 25 percent.[16] Workers fled to Europe and South America in search of work. Employers struck back at striking workers by hiring the most recent immigrants.[17] "The 1873 depression was felt throughout the entire industrial sector, and production, employment, and income fell sharply everywhere. The dollar value of business failures in 1873 was greater than in any other single year between 1857 and 1893. Deflation in the iron and steel industry was especially severe: 266 of the nation's 666 iron furnaces were out of blast by January 1, 1874, and more than 50 percent of the rail mills were silent."[18]

With the depression in full throttle, the *Commercial and Financial Chronicle* reported to its capitalist readers in 1877 that "labor is under control for the first time since the [Civil] war." In this context, laborers leveraged the only thing left to them — their labor. They withheld it and catapulted the first mass strike into the history pages of the United States. By so doing, they fundamentally challenged the railroad industry — the most powerful business of that day.

After a six-year effort, the transcontinental railroad was completed in 1869, knitting together far-flung states and territories. Similar to the Internet of today, the nationwide web of railroad tracks made it possible for people of power and people of even meager means to communicate and create new communities where none had existed before. The telegraph wires that accompanied thousands of miles of track also prefigured the Internet — post upon post upholding the glass insulators that cradled the wires that connected a continent. Each year from 1865 until the Panic of 1873 witnessed the construction of thousands of miles of new

---

16. Jeremy Brecher, *Strike!* rev. ed. (Boston: South End Press, 1997), 10.

17. Howard Zinn, *A People's History of the United States* (New York: HarperPerennial, 1990), 238–39.

18. Herbert G. Gutman, "The Workers' Search for Power: Labor in the Gilded Age," in *Power and Culture: Essays on the American Working Class*, ed. Ira Berlin (New York: Pantheon, 1987), 74.

track. Over seven thousand miles were laid down in 1871 alone.[19] As Stephen Ambrose notes, in his railroad-baron-friendly hagiography on the building of the transcontinental railroad, this railroad made a nation-wide stock market and a continent-wide economy and culture possible. "A continent-wide culture in which mail and popular magazines and books that used to cost dollars per ounce and had taken forever to get from the East to the West Coast now cost pennies and got there in a few days."[20] Another historian notes that the railroad enabled whole cities to take up specialties. "Chicago turned hog butcher for the nation, Minneapolis became the nation's miller, Lynn its cobbler, Paterson spun its silk, St. Louis brewed its beer. Railroads made possible that triumph of mass production and marketing."[21] No wonder then that "when the railroads shivered, the nation shook."[22]

The railroad barons and political elite did not shiver because of the cold in the long hot summer of 1877. Rather it was for a singular event in the history of labor in the United States. Known variously by historians as the Great Railroad Strike, the Great Upheaval, the Great Uprising of 1877, and the Great Strikes of 1877, the strikes that summer remain the most militant and widespread in the country's history.[23]

The economic depression that followed the Panic of 1873 and the overall disastrous state of the union movement provided the occasion for railroad magnates to slash wages and hold off wage payments. Rail work-ers had already endured cuts of up to 60 percent since the beginning of the depression.[24] Before the wage cuts, brakemen, who performed one of the most dangerous jobs in the industry, averaged $1.75 per twelve-hour day. Conductors averaged around $2.78 and firemen around $1.90.[25] Scheduled monthly wage payments could be up to four months late. At times, work weeks were only three or four days in length. Other troubles included layovers when a one-way trip required that a worker, at his

---

19. Robert V. Bruce, *1877: Year of Violence* (Indianapolis: Bobbs-Merrill, 1959), 32.

20. Stephen E. Ambrose, *Nothing Like It in the World: The Men Who Built the Transcontinental Railroad, 1863–1869* (New York: Simon & Schuster, 2000), 370.

21. Bruce, *1877: Year of Violence*, 31.

22. Ibid., 29.

23. The assessment of the extent of these strikes is from Philip S. Foner, *From Colonial Times to the Founding of the American Federation of Labor,* vol. 1 of *History of the Labor Movement in the United States* (New York: International Publishers, 1982), 464.

24. Priscilla Murolo and A. B. Chitty, *From the Folks Who Brought You the Weekend: A Short, Illustrated History of Labor in the United States* (New York: New Press, 2001), 105.

25. Bruce, *1877: Year of Violence*, 44, 46.

own expense, wait until a work-related trip could get him home again.[26] Company hotels charged the exorbitant rate of a dollar a night on wages that totaled between five and ten dollars a week.[27] Workdays could be fourteen hours long.[28] A job classification system that held down wages added to the workers' grievances.[29] Unionized workers were blacklisted and railway companies spied on workers and their organizations through the services of the hated Pinkerton detectives.

The straw that nearly broke the nation's back that summer was set down when the Pennsylvania Railroad declared a wage cut of 10 percent to take effect on June 1. This affected the workers on the sixty-six hundred miles of track that it owned outright, controlled, or operated. Three other railroads, the Baltimore & Ohio, the Northern Pacific, and the Chicago, Burlington & Quincy also cut rates but waited until after July 1. In Allegheny City, across the river from Pittsburgh, on June 2, 1877, railroad employees met to form the Trainmen's Union to consist of engineers (the elite among trainmen), conductors, firemen, brakemen, switchmen, and other workers.[30] The goal was to unify railroad laborers in a concerted manner to counter the railroad magnates. One estimate is that thousands of workers were organized in only three weeks with nearly five hundred in Pittsburgh alone.[31]

The first action of note for the Trainmen's Union occurred on July 16, when forty B&O freight train firemen and brakemen stopped work and halted a freight train just outside Baltimore.[32] Strikebreakers and local police quickly quelled this effort by the Baltimore section of this new union. Also, on the same day, in Martinsburg, West Virginia, an important junction of the B&O, twelve hundred brakemen and firemen seized the depot, roadhouse, and machine shops. They halted all trains and demanded that the 10 percent pay cut be rescinded. After local officials refused to confront the crowds, railroad officials called on Governor H. M. Matthews to send in the West Virginia militia. The militia put in a half-hearted and failed effort to disperse the strikers. In frustration, John

26. Ibid., 47.

27. Foner, *From Colonial Times to the Founding of the American Federation of Labor,* 464.

28. Paul Le Blanc, *A Short History of the U.S. Working Class: From Colonial Times to the Twenty-first Century* (Amherst, N.Y.: Humanity Books, an imprint of Prometheus Books, 1999), 45.

29. Brecher, *Strike!* 17.

30. Bruce, *1877: Year of Violence,* 59.

31. Ibid., 61.

32. Foner, *From Colonial Times to the Founding of the American Federation of Labor,* 465.

Garrett, head of the B&O, asked the governor to call the president to mobilize federal troops. The governor first tried yet other divisions of the state militia, which likewise failed to stop the strike. This second failure of the state militia, and Garrett's unremitting pressure, finally prompted the governor to telegram President Rutherford B. Hayes to send in federal troops. On July 19, over three hundred federal troops and officers arrived and participated in the second ever peacetime suppression of a strike. (Andrew Jackson sent in federal troops in 1834 to put down a labor dispute with workers at the Chesapeake and Ohio Canal.) The strikers had strategically scattered in anticipation of the arrival of the troops and the blockade was broken. It seemed as if the strike was over. But in a pattern that would be repeated that year, other workers joined in. Outside of town, hundreds of unemployed and striking boatmen of the Chesapeake and Ohio Canal stopped a westbound freight train that did manage to get out of Martinsburg.[33]

When the strike broke out again in Baltimore on July 20, more violence ensued. Garrett of the B&O worked his way with yet another public official, Governor Carroll of Maryland. The Maryland National Guard was mobilized and instructed to go to nearby Cumberland, where unemployed and migrant workers, boatmen, and young boys stopped trains coming out of Martinsburg. The Guard's first task was simply to get to the train station in Baltimore and then travel by rail to Cumberland. This part of their "commute" put the Guard in direct confrontation with an angry populace and an agitated workforce sympathetic to the efforts in Cumberland and Martinsburg. The militia killed ten men and boys and seriously wounded more than twenty.[34] The destruction of a moderate amount of railroad property, the massing of over fifteen thousand protesters, and the possibility of additional violence resulted in President Hayes sending federal troops to Maryland (in addition to the ones already in West Virginia). The militia never made it to Cumberland that day. By Sunday, July 22, however, five hundred federal troops were in Baltimore, and though passenger train service resumed, the freight train strike endured.[35] These strikes energized still other workers on other railway lines in Pennsylvania, New York, New Jersey, Ohio, Illinois, Missouri, and California to take up job actions.

33. From Bruce, *1877: Year of Violence*, chapter 5, "First Blood," 74–92.

34. Ibid., 108.

35. From Bruce, *1877: Year of Violence*, chapter 6, "The Bell Tolls in Baltimore," 93–114.

When the strikes spread to Pittsburgh, the resulting violence was unprecedented. The pay cuts were bad enough for the workers there, but the order from the Pennsylvania Railroad that *all* eastbound freight trains out of Pittsburgh had to be "double-headers" (with two locomotives) was the breaking point. This meant that one crew would no longer handle eighteen cars but up to thirty-six. More work, less pay, more injuries, and half the number of conductors and brakemen would be the results. The catalyst for Pittsburgh's eruption of violence was the simple refusal of train workers to acquiesce to these latest demands and threats to their livelihood. The Trainmen's Union helped to organize the workers and one often quoted worker from a rolling mill declared in solidarity: "We're with you, we're in the same boat. I heard a reduction of ten per cent hinted at in our mill this morning. I won't call employers despots, I won't call them tyrants, but the term capitalists is sort of synonymous and will do as well."[36]

By July 21, it was clear that the local Pittsburgh militia would be a useless force to dislodge local miners and railway workers who had by then idled two thousand freight cars and locomotives. Governor Hartranft of Pennsylvania ordered the Philadelphia militia to go to Pittsburgh. This militia fired into the crowd of workers and spectators and killed twenty men, women, and children and wounded twenty-nine others. An outraged city rose up. Six hundred workers from a neighboring town marched over to help. Other crowd members assembled into small military units. The Philadelphia militia retreated. Since they lacked the authority from local officials to continue the fight and given the merciful reluctance of the Philadelphia officers to use their own Gatling guns, the militia holed up in railroad buildings. These buildings were located downhill and reachable on tracks by scores of loaded oil and coal cars.

The inevitable occurred. Burning railway cars were aimed at the militia and the railroad headquarters. Many claimed then that officials of the railroad took advantage of the chaos and ordered this assault to gain sympathy and eventual insurance payments. In a mass frenzy of fury and retaliation that continued into Sunday, July 22, the carnage had warlike proportions. According to Mother Jones's vivid account, "It was a wild night. The flames lighted the sky and turned to fiery flames the steel bayonets of the soldiers."[37] When the sun rose on Monday, a two-

---

36. Bruce, *1877: Year of Violence*, 125.
37. Jones, *The Autobiography of Mother Jones*, 15.

mile stretch of Pittsburgh was in complete ruin. In all, 104 locomotives and 2,152 rail cars that could have stretched out over eleven miles were destroyed. In addition to the property of the railroad including the roundhouses, sheds, depot, and other offices, seventy-nine other build-ings in Pittsburgh were reduced to ashes. Carloads of scrap hauled away from the scene totaled twelve hundred. Twenty-four people were killed in the violence, including four soldiers from Philadelphia.[38]

The panic fanned outward to New York City and Washington, D.C. One newspaper in New York City reported that Pittsburgh was in the power of a "howling mob," and another paper called for "a diet of lead for hungry strikers." Others compared the events to the Paris Commune six years earlier. President Rutherford B. Hayes called out federal troops to protect Washington. His cabinet proposed to declare the whole of Pennsylvania in insurrection.[39] In neighboring Allegheny, strikers took over the armory, the telegraph office, and management of the railroad. One account goes so far as to say that the Allegheny workers had effec-tively seized "economic management and political power" there.[40] Strikes spread to other Pennsylvania towns including Columbia, Meadville, and Chenago, and strikers seized railroads and stopped troop movements.

In many locations, the railway strikes led to general strikes which in-dicated that the working class viewed this as a common struggle against employers.[41] Spurred on by the events in Pittsburgh, the neighboring town of McKeesport saw employees from the National Tube Works, steel-workers employed by Andrew Carnegie, and hundreds of laborers from a number of industries participate in a general strike with calls for raises in pay. General strikes spread to Harrisburg, Pennsylvania, to Zanesville, Columbia, and Toledo, Ohio, and to San Francisco (though the strike there was marred by attacks on Chinese workers). In Chicago, trans-portation and industry was shut down, and crowds forced stockyard and gaswork officials to promise in writing that wages would be raised to two dollars a day.[42] Black workers galvanized white workers in Galve-ston, Texas, into action that resulted in raising the standard wage to two dollars. In Louisville, Kentucky, black sanitation workers joined in and urged strikes to get wages to $1.50 a day. Coopers, textile workers,

38. Bruce, *1877: Year of Violence*, 180.
39. Foner, *From Colonial Times to the Founding of the American Federation of Labor*, 468.
40. Brecher, *Strike!* 27.
41. Ibid., 29.
42. Ibid., 30–31.

plow factory workers, brick makers, and cabinet workers joined the general strike.[43] Even before Pittsburgh's flames burned brightest, Newark, Ohio, and Hornellsville, New York, both saw confrontations with local militia.

The St. Louis Citywide Strike

The most significant developments of 1877 occurred in St. Louis. The troubles of the railway workers certainly set events in motion, but the citywide strike that occurred there and the power of the Executive Committee that helped organize it stands out in a year of outstanding events. According to David T. Burbank's account of the events that summer, the systematic shutdown of all the city's industry fully justifies the use of the term "general strike." In his estimation, no other city came as close to St. Louis did to being ruled by a workers' soviet.[44]

While Pittsburgh was a flaming beacon to worker unrest on Sunday, July 22, railroad workers in East St. Louis, a modest city of nine thousand in Illinois and home to the second most important railroad center in the west after Chicago, issued General Order No. 1. All freight traffic would cease, though passenger and mail cars would be allowed through. This mass meeting consisted of rail workers from seven different rail lines. Representatives from the St. Louis Workingmen's Party were also in attendance.[45]

The actions in East St. Louis energized workers in St. Louis and Carondelet to the south. A meeting on Monday night in Carondelet of railroad workers and Vulcan Iron Works employees may have been the first step toward the general strike in St. Louis.[46] In downtown St. Louis, at Lucas Market, another mass meeting of up to five thousand workers occurred that evening, organized by the St. Louis Executive Committee. By Tuesday, the general strike was in progress in St. Louis. Coopers in fife and drum went from shop to shop shouting, "Come out, come out!" Some St. Louis Gas Works employees did come out. Boatmen and newsboys stopped work. Engineers on river boats won wage increases.[47] By

---

43. Ibid., 32.
44. David T. Burbank, *Reign of the Rabble: The St. Louis General Strike of 1877* (New York: Augustus M. Kelley Publishers, 1966), 2.
45. Ibid., 15–17.
46. Ibid., 31.
47. Ibid., 43.

Wednesday, the general strike had peaked. Freight service was cut off to the East.[48] That morning, white and black boat workers won wage increases; still other crews left their jobs. Black boat workers joined the march.[49] The Merchants' Exchange was shut down and the mayor urged all business concerns to close so that employers and employees could enroll in the citizens' militia to counter the striking workers.[50] The Executive Committee themselves had already identified factories, shops, and businesses to be closed down. The march of five thousand workers paraded through St. Louis and successfully appealed to workers in foundries, bagging companies, flour mills, bakeries, and chemical, zinc, and lead works to stop production.[51] The procession was led by strikers bearing a loaf of bread on a flag staff, the red flag of the international workers' movement fluttered freely, and a brass band struck up the Marseillaise every so often as they marched. Seeing the bread held aloft, marchers cheered and shouted, "This is what we are fighting for!" and "Let it be the symbol of the strike!"[52] Meanwhile in East St. Louis, women joined in a parade to the Relay Station in support of the strike. A proclamation, in English and German, stated the demands:

> We recommend a general strike of all branches of industry for eight hours as a day's work, and we call on the legislature for the immediate enactment of an eight hour law, and the enforcement of a severe penalty for its violation, and that the employment of all children under fourteen years of age be prohibited. *Resolved*, that it is our purpose never to give up the strike till these propositions are enforced. The Executive Committee.[53]

A sense of the urgency is captured in this assessment of the events that day: "On the evening of Wednesday, July 25, 1877, public officials throughout the United States felt more genuine alarm at the possibility of imminent social revolution than on any occasion before or since."[54] In sum, for a short time, the St. Louis Executive Committee controlled the city. Rail traffic moved, but it was within the authority of the workers

---

48. Ibid., 69.
49. Ibid., 71.
50. Ibid., 66.
51. Ibid., 71–76.
52. Ibid., 75.
53. *Proclamation*, St. Louis, Missouri, July 25, 1877. Burbank, facing the title page.
54. Ibid., 87.

who operated the trains and collected fares. In a stunning reversal of power, the owner of the Belcher Sugar Refinery approached the Committee for permission to operate his own plant in order to prevent food spoilage. Meanwhile, railroad officials wanted the workers to be treated as if they were waging war against the United States.[55]

While authorities at all levels had St. Louis and its Executive Committee in view, it was hard to stay focussed on any one place for long. After all, at the same time twenty thousand workers were marching through Chicago with banners proclaiming, "We want work not charity," "Why does overproduction cause starvation?" "Life by work or death by fight." Citizens' patrols, police, and federal troops broke up the strike; thirty to fifty people were killed and nearly one hundred were wounded.[56]

Worker "control" of St. Louis turned out to be temporary. While the Executive Committee was holding rallies and conducting marches and issuing demands, authorities at the local, state, and federal level were planning to take back St. Louis. This was accomplished with much fanfare but little bloodshed. On Friday, July 27, the state militia and police broke the strike with the takeover of Schuler Hall, the headquarters of the Committee. A day later, federal troops returned control to the authorities in East St. Louis. The Executive Committee's plan of holding off a military confrontation, strengthening their own forces, negotiating settlements with employers, and peacefully closing out the general strike was thwarted.

The end of the St. Louis general strike marked the turning point in the "war" that year. The physical impact was enormous. "When the great railroad strikes of 1877 were over, a hundred people were dead, a thousand people had gone to jail, 100,000 workers had gone on strike, and the strikes had roused into action countless unemployed in the cities. More than half the freight on the nation's 75,000 miles of track had stopped running at the height of the strikes."[57] Other assessments of the great upheavals that year vary. One could argue that the movement was a failure because the strikes were crushed. Still, the strikes halted the hitherto unchallenged unilateral cuts in wages by railway officials. This concerted action did encourage more worker involvement in unions than

---

55. Ibid., 88.
56. Foner, *From Colonial Times to the Founding of the American Federation of Labor,* 470–71.
57. Zinn, *A People's History of the United States,* 246.

had been attempted in the years prior to 1877.[58] The *Iron Age*, a manufacturers' journal, noted that "the reduction in the wages of labor has reached its lowest point.... It would be a bold step in a wrong direction to give notice of a decrease in wages."[59] Overall, the events of that year reminded capitalists that however much they wished to avoid laborers and their concerns, such matters could not be ignored.

Washington Gladden

As an early advocate of social Christianity, Washington Gladden set the tone for many Protestant Christians regarding the relations between labor and capital. *Working People and Their Employers* was published in 1876, and it has been long recognized as "one of the first mileposts set by American social Christianity."[60] He served as pastor in Springfield, Massachusetts, and wrote this book while the country was reeling from the Panic of 1873. He finished just before the events of 1877.

The lifting of the depression or simple reforms in the wage system would not be enough, according to Gladden, to reverse the fundamental ills besetting both workers and capitalists. He looked to history and argued that there is "something better" than the wage system.[61] While unions could effect positive change by turning back the abuses that prevailed under the wage system, true social reform and solidarity would forever remain unattainable without looking beyond them to a cooperative system where all would share in the wealth of production. A system of cooperation would entail basic respect and dignity for the workers. Cooperation was a two-way street which meant moving beyond the "heartless and extortionate" employers *and* "greedy and headstrong" employees.[62] "If the capitalist would measure his profits, and the workingman his wages, by the Golden Rule, there would be instant peace."[63] Labor and capital would not be separated by the "intervention of corporations, or through the building up of immense industrial concerns by individuals or firms" if employers were concerned to govern themselves

58. Burbank, *Reign of the Rabble,* 188.

59. Bruce, *1877: Year of Violence,* 302.

60. C. H. Hopkins, *The Rise of the Social Gospel in American Protestantism, 1865–1915* (New Haven: Yale University Press, 1940), 27.

61. Washington Gladden, *Working People and Their Employers* (Boston: Lockwood, Brooks, and Company, 1876), 44.

62. Ibid., 39.

63. Ibid., 43.

by the Christian law.[64] True cooperation in the economy can be connected with the major image of Christianity — the body of Christ. "For,
let no one fail to see that co-operation is nothing more than the arrangement of the essential factors of industry according to the Christian rule,
'We being many are one body in Christ, and every one members one of
another.' It is capital and labor adjusting themselves to the form of Christianity."[65] The connection of the theme of cooperation with the image
of the body is an important and recurring feature of Gladden's work.

The point about societal structure was posed again in *Applied Christianity* (1886). His conception of the organic character of society is based
on the assumption that society is a "natural" phenomenon that is fundamentally about order. Society is threatened to the core when it ignores
one of its constituent elements. He believed that the industrial system is
based on a "social solecism."[66] To "hold society together upon an anti-
social foundation" is impossible.[67] His indictment of the present system
was stinging: "To bring capitalists and laborers together in an association,
and set them over against each other, and announce to them the principle of competition as the guide of their conduct, bidding each party to
get as much as it can out of the other, and to give as little as it can, — for
that is precisely what competition means, — is simply to declare war —
a war in which the strongest will win."[68]

Gladden's view of industrial relationships is based on his belief in
"the absolute unity of human interests."[69] If we are truly "members one
of another," it would be "just as rational for the right hand and the left
hand to fly at each other, and beat and bruise each other till one or
the other was disabled, as it is for employer and employed to fall into
contention and controversy."[70] The unity of human interests precluded
the possibility on moral grounds that one social class may "rise up" if it
means that another social class should fall. If any "one member of the
social organism suffers all the other members must suffer with it."[71] Man-

---

64. Ibid., 171–72.

65. Ibid., 50.

66. Washington Gladden, *Applied Christianity: Moral Aspects of Social Questions* (Boston:
Houghton, Mifflin, 1894), 32.

67. Ibid., 32–33.

68. Ibid., 33.

69. Washington Gladden, *Tools and the Man: Property and Industry under the Christian
Law* (Boston: Houghton, Mifflin, 1893), 179.

70. Ibid., 178–79.

71. Ibid., 179.

agement and owners must not plunder the wealth of the workers, and workers must not presume that their labor is the sole cause of the wealth of the enterprise. Both are to work together as brothers and partners in business. To continue with strikes, lockouts, blacklisting, boycotting is not only to be engaged in human conflict but to be involved in fighting "against the stars in their courses, against the Ruler of the universe."[72] Not only is this wicked, but it is "absurd, unnatural and monstrous."[73]

Gladden's extended explanation of industrial partnerships in *Tools and the Man* (1893) begins with a short discussion on the merits and pitfalls of arbitration as a method for adjusting labor disputes. He believed that arbitration is the "word of the hour," though it should not be considered the last word. It is merely the next stage of development beyond the strikes and lockouts that are "characteristics of the feudal age of labor and capital."[74] The point of arbitration is to dampen the division, to hold the line on strife and fighting over the spoils by appealing to reason rather than force. But even arbitration does not deal with the root causes of industrial strife and thus highlights the advantages of industrial partnerships.

> Under this system, the capital is furnished and the business is organized and directed by the employer: the workmen are paid wages at the market rate, and at the end of the year a stipulated percentage of the net profits is divided among them, each man's dividend being proportioned to the amount of his earnings. . . . This plan makes the workmen partners in the business; they are not merely "hands," they are associates; their eyes and their brains and their hearts are enlisted as well as their hands; their interests are identified with those of the employer; the larger the gains of the business are, the larger their share will be.[75]

The introduction of industrial partnerships entails participation. He believed that, in the present stage of industrial evolution, partnership and participation had become expedient and imperative. In any event, industrial partnerships are attempts to organize labor according to Christian law. Gladden had advice for both employers and employees on this

---

72. Ibid., 181.
73. Ibid.
74. Ibid., 205.
75. Ibid., 209.

matter. Employers must remember that industry is an association, a so-cial organization that calls for an altruistic element. "Society cannot be built on the basis of commercial contract. You who gather men together for these great industries have constant need to remember these words of Carlyle: 'Love of men cannot be bought by cash-payment; and without love men cannot endure to be together.' "[76] He considered this work an opportunity of Christian leadership and "statesmanship" and, in an ap-parent nod to the Knights of Labor, noted that "Knightlier work can no man do than that which awaits them."[77] As for workers, he urged them to consider that "men are not all alike." Services rendered to society are not alike and so the rewards cannot be the same either. The coordinat-ing function (management) is useful and costly. Those who provide it deserve greater rewards. This is an eternal law and socialistic schemes that ignore it will only come to grief.

Other Voices for Labor Peace

The 1880s marked a major turning point in U.S. labor history. The extraordinary expansion of capitalism during this decade and the back-lashes it provoked continue to provide fodder for labor historians and anyone concerned with the intersection of economics and violence. The agitation for the eight-hour day, the Haymarket Massacre of 1886, the meteoric rise and fall of the Knights of Labor, and the rise of the Ameri-can Federation of Labor punctuate a very lively decade. While the 1880s do not have the record for the sheer number of strikes, there was a steady and uninterrupted rise in the number of strikes and the laborers involved. Almost half of the strikes between 1881 and 1886 occurred without union approval or aid.[78] In these years, over thirty-nine hundred strikes in over twenty-two thousand establishments idled more than 1.3 million workers.[79] These events shook the nation, according to some his-torians, more profoundly than even 1877. In 1886 alone, the number of strikes doubled from the year before. Between 1881 and 1894, more than four million workers were involved in over fourteen thousand strikes and other labor-management struggles. As in 1877, the agitation for shorter workdays was a major theme of the struggles. On May 1, 1886, nearly

---

76. Ibid., 237.
77. Ibid., 238.
78. Montgomery, *Workers' Control in America,* 18–20.
79. Brecher, *Strike!* 47.

a half million marchers across the country turned out for the first May Day, the international workers' holiday.[80]

While the streets were lively, authors were agitating for change in their own way. Several books published in that decade rattled both academics and the general public in a way that continues to impress observers of this period of U.S. history. These include Henry George's *Progress and Poverty* (with the first edition commercially available in 1880), Laurence Gronlund's *The Coöperative Commonwealth* (1884), and Edward Bellamy's *Looking Backward* (1888). No account of the economic history of the 1880s in the United States would be complete without examining the impact these books had across a broad spectrum of the U.S. populace. George's proposal for the "single tax" on unearned increments on the value of land, Gronlund's vision of a "future Social Order...in which all important instruments of production have been taken under collective control," and Bellamy's blueprint for collectivism in his popular *Looking Backward* were important events in a decade that also witnessed the virtual overnight collapse of the Knights of Labor.[81] In 1886, an early historian of labor in the United States, George E. McNeill, editor of *The Labor Movement: The Problem of Today,* concluded: "When the Golden Rule of Christ shall measure the relations of men in all their duties...in factory and workshop, in the mine, in the field, in commerce...the promise of the prophet and the poet shall be fulfilled...and peace on earth shall prevail."[82]

In addition to Gladden, other Protestant social Christians tried to cool the heated passions over equity and control in the workplace so that something like a "cooperative commonwealth" might emerge. In 1888, Reverend Harry W. Cadman of San Francisco won $1,000 for his efforts as the author of *The Christian Unity of Capital and Labor* from the American Sunday School Union. He called upon the wealthy to consider the ethics of Christianity. In words that anticipate a contemporary covenantal ethic, he noted that a "cold compliance with the letter of the contract made with labor is not the acquittance that Christianity demands. The payment of wages on Saturday does not absolve the payer from his week's obligation. Above and beyond is a great stewardship of

---

80. Philip S. Foner, *May Day: A Short History of the International Workers' Holiday, 1886–1986* (New York: International Publishers, 1986), 27.

81. Laurence Gronlund, *The Cooperative Commonwealth* (Cambridge: The Belknap Press of Harvard University Press, 1965), 90.

82. Hopkins, *The Rise of the Social Gospel in American Protestantism, 1865–1915,* 88.

which none can divest themselves."[83] Cooperation between labor and management is possible and ultimately profitable because everyone's interests and duties are in harmony with everyone else. For Cadman, strikes and lockouts prove nothing but the superior force of the victor.[84] They often fail and they are inefficient. But when all arbitration fails, then Christianity does not require that labor give up its divine and natural right to self-protection. Strikes are not ultimately impermissible.[85] He concludes that Christianity desires to "complete its triumphs" by working toward "bonds of conciliation." Once it has carried itself to every relation of labor and capital and demonstrated its ability to bring a harmony to opposites, then the gospel will be viewed as "a religion fitted for to-day, and that *it will answer* the social problems of to-day, whether propounded by workman, employer, or consumer."[86]

Walter Rauschenbusch

Walter Rauschenbusch is known for his advocacy of cooperation within "practical socialism" or cooperative experimentation. But he also reflected at length on the cooperative achievements within capitalism itself. Capitalism depends upon cooperation. It would have no strength and no value unless it could usefully combine "many units of capital in the financing of an industrial undertaking, and many units of labor in the operation of it."[87] To the extent that this happens within a business, this is morally good. The problems come when the interest of one business collides with that of another. In such instances, "all the virtues and the vices of war are developed."[88] Cooperation, on the other hand, promotes good will and solidarity. It makes Christian love natural and spontaneous. "Thus coöperation is both moral and efficient. If it were not economically efficient, it would not be moral; if it were not moral, it would not be permanently efficient."[89]

83. H. W. Cadman, *The Christian Unity of Capital and Labor* (Philadelphia: American Sunday School Union, 1888), 103.

84. Ibid., 160.

85. Ibid., 243.

86. Ibid., 253.

87. Walter Rauschenbusch, *Christianizing the Social Order* (New York: Macmillan, 1921; originally published 1912), 170.

88. Ibid., 171.

89. Ibid., 170.

The recognition that cooperation should be the basic requirement for capitalism did not mean that capitalism in the United States somehow fulfilled the ideals of the cooperative commonwealth. Far from it. As he pointed out in *Christianity and the Social Crisis*, capitalism necessarily divides industrial society into two classes — those who own the "instruments and materials" of production and those who provide their labor. He claimed that such a division, the peculiar characteristic of modern capitalism, forces the classes to cooperate if there is to be any production at all. Labor was always in an inferior position. "It has to wrestle on its knees with a foeman [sic] who is on his feet. Is this unequal struggle between two conflicting interests to go on forever? Is this insecurity the best that the working class can ever hope to attain?"[90]

The transition from competitive business practices to cooperative ones must not be achieved by the use of force. The only way that the labor movement will be able to achieve this transition is through different alliances. The first is an alliance with religion — those who support the "Christian principle of brotherly association." Labor needs the "high elation and faith" that comes with religion.[91] The second alliance that workers need in the gradual and evolutionary shift to socialism anticipates contemporary employee participation programs:

> The cooperation of professional men outside the working class would contribute scientific information and trained intelligence. They would mediate between the two classes, interpreting each to the other, and thereby lessening the strain of hostility. Their presence and sympathy would cheer the working people and diminish the sense of class isolation. By their contact with the possessing classes they could help to persuade them of the inherent justice of the labor movement and so create a leaning toward concessions. No other influence could do so much to prevent a revolutionary explosion of pent-up forces.[92]

His appeal to "scientific information" and "trained intelligence" is reminiscent of Gladden's wish for trained capitalists to teach workers the way of workplace organization and efficient, profit-producing enterprises. Yet Rauschenbusch is looking to something else. While his dominant

---

90. Walter Rauschenbusch, *Christianity and the Social Crisis* (Louisville: Westminster/John Knox Press, 1991; originally published 1907), 407.
91. Ibid., 409.
92. Ibid., 409–10.

concern is with the possibilities of cooperative fraternity over economic individualism, in this section of *Christianity and the Social Crisis,* he is concerned to prevent the sudden seizure of power by the working class. If this were to happen, the laboring class might well get "beaten back with terrible loss in efficiency to the movement."[93] Worse yet, there would be widespread disorder with a "reactionary" relapse to the old ways. Better that each side should agree to a gradual shift in power or what he calls "a continuous series of practicable demands on one side and concessions on the other."[94] If professional and business classes can overcome selfish interests on their own, this lessens the chances of violence and the results of pent-up anger and frustration on the part of the working class.

Federal Council of the Churches of Christ in America

The founding of the Federal Council of the Churches of Christ in America in 1908 was a landmark event in the history of Protestantism in the United States. Thirty-three denominations came together to form the Federal Council, representing nearly eighteen million people. The emphasis of the Federal Council was "Christian activity" and not the reconciliation of divergent doctrinal issues. Its constitution denied it "authority to draw up a common creed, form of government, or worship."[95] The report of the Committee on the Church and Modern Industry presented by Rev. Frank Mason North (secretary of the National City Evangelization Union of the Methodist Episcopal Church) is an important example of the Federal Council's decision to highlight matters of social concern. The delegates' unanimous adoption of "The Church and Modern Industry" was an important historical breakthrough for U.S. Protestantism because it "achieved the long-hoped-for official response of Protestant Christianity to the crisis in the social order, [and] it also provided a visible symbol of that commitment."[96]

It is necessary to review "The Church and Modern Industry" report to provide a reading on the attitudes and views of institutionalized Protestantism on labor at the beginning of this century. The report repudiates

---

93. Ibid., 410.

94. Ibid.

95. Edward L. Queen II, "National Council of Churches," in *The Encyclopedia of American Religious History,* ed. Edward L. Queen II, Stephen R. Prothero, Gardiner H. Shattuck Jr. (New York: Facts on File, 1996), 436.

96. Donald K. Gorrell, *The Age of Social Responsibility: The Social Gospel in the Progressive Era, 1900–1920* (Macon, Ga.: Mercer University Press, 1988), 111.

a "class gospel" and any attempt to deal with society on a "class basis." Christ's authority and his example is such that the Gospel message goes to "men as men" and not to "laborers" or "capitalists." According to the report, the church of Christ recognizes only two categories: those who follow Christ and those who do not. The church is meant to be a benefactor of all classes.

While the Federal Council's document resists explicit appeals to "class" as a way of describing the relation of Christianity to the labor question, it does not repudiate the need for "workingmen" to organize for "social and industrial betterment." In fact, such activity belongs to the "natural order" and the effort to secure better work conditions is evidence of God's call to share in the "higher experiences" of the intellectual and spiritual life. The church must cease from any talk about "conceding" the right to union organizing. It must welcome its exercise since it is already "in the nature of things." As long as unions avoid practices that create industrial havoc, they must be accepted as allies of the church. Unions must attend to immediate difficulties, yet their chief responsibility is "the creation of that atmosphere of fairness, kindness and good will, in which those who contend, employer and employee, capitalist and workingman, may find both light and warmth, and, in mutual respect and with fraternal feelings, may reach the common basis of understanding which will come to them not by outward pressure, but from the inner sense of brotherhood."[97] Capitalists also have a "natural right" to organize themselves for their ends. Whether it is capital or labor, "social bewilderment" must be met by "ethical lucidity" and the test for right conduct can only be measured by gentle and resolute appeals to the truth of the whole Gospel.

The "Statement and Resolutions" section emphasized that the complex problems of modern industry could be "interpreted and solved only by the teachings of the New Testament, and that Jesus Christ is final authority in the social as in the individual life."[98] Since the obligations of industry involve employer and employee, society and government, and rich and poor — tolerance, patience, and mutual confidence must be the watchwords. From the perspective of labor-management relations, the heart of the report is contained in the sixth subsection of the statement

---

97. Elias B. Sanford, ed., *Report of the First Meeting of the Federal Council* (Philadelphia, 1908), Federal Council of the Churches of Christ in America (New York: Revell Press, 1909), 235.

98. Ibid., 236.

section. Employers who exhibit "fraternal spirit" by, among other good deeds, instituting profit-sharing and submitting differences to arbitration should be praised. Labor organizations deserve "admiration" when they promote temperate views among their members, increase efficiency, and set "the example of calmness and self-restraint in conference with employers."[99] When such behavior is mandated by unions, this is proof that the labor movement is ethical in its fundamental purposes.

> We note as omens of industrial peace and goodwill, the growth of a spirit of conciliation, and of the practice of conference and arbitration in settling trade disputes. We trust profoundly that these methods may supplant those of the strike and the lockout, the boycott and the black list. Lawlessness and violence on either side of labor controversies are an invasion of the rights of the people and must be condemned and resisted. We believe no better opportunity could be afforded to Christian men, employers and wage-earners alike, to rebuke the superciliousness of power and the obstinacy of opinion, than by asserting and illustrating before their fellows in labor contests, the Gospel which deals with men as men and has for its basis of fraternity the Golden Rule. We commend most heartily the societies and leagues in which employers and workingmen come together upon a common platform to consider the problems of each in the interest of both, and we urge Christian men more freely to participate in such movements of conciliation.[100]

The report concludes by noting that the strength of the church rests not in a program but in matters of the Spirit. The church is not a school or a legislature or a court. It is not given any function except for the one of revealing the "ethical and practical values of a spiritual faith." The job of the church is not to lay the foundations of the social order. It is to reveal or disclose the already existing basis for society. Furthermore, the church is to create a spirit of brotherhood so that the truths which can shape industrial relations may become operative. The sympathy, love, and sacrifice of Jesus Christ is the standard by which the church should compare its efforts.

---

99. Ibid., 237.
100. Ibid., 238.

"The Church and Modern Industry" is an expression of the "state of the question" on labor issues and the Protestant church at the beginning of the twentieth century. The fact that the report and the newly formed Federal Council granted any attention to the cause of labor was an important step for a Protestant church that had allowed "estrangement between the Church and the industrial workers." While the claim that workers have a "natural" right to organize is not explained or defended in any way, it too can be recognized as a positive step even in the face of the simultaneous delegitimization of any discussion about class. This report shows the typical social gospel overconfidence in the efficacy of simple appeals to moral norms to solve industrial problems. No recognition is given to the relative weakness of labor in the face of capital. The entire report assumed that labor and capital were on equal footing and had equal opportunity to inflict damage on each other. It also assumed that both parties had an equal interest in preventing such violence in order to maintain their viability. On the other hand, the report contained the "Social Creed," which was an explicit witness to the very serious conditions that faced the average laborer at that time. Had it been taken seriously, a much more militant approach to the labor question than what is contained in the rest of the report would have been necessary.

Conclusion

This review of moments of nineteenth-century labor history and selected social gospel responses to the trials of the day reveals similarities with the contemporary covenantal business viewpoints on the workplace. Rauschenbusch's concern about the backlash from revolutionary activity and the need for labor and management to make reasonable demands and timely concessions is reminiscent of Stewart Herman's contemporary call for the self-binding activities that labor and management should undertake to reduce their antagonisms. Herman's injunction that management and employees need to be mutually accountable on the basis of shared restraint in the use of power is part of a long tradition in Protestant Christianity of holding both sides equally accountable.[101]

---

101. Stewart W. Herman, *Durable Goods: A Covenantal Ethic for Management and Employees* (Notre Dame, Ind.: University of Notre Dame Press, 1997), 4.

The story told in chapter 5 shows the history of corporate attempts to undermine independent unions and union-organizing. It is a difficult history of corporate betrayal and subterfuge to keep workers off balance and unable to determine for themselves their own direction and priorities in the workplace. The call for mutual accountability of unions and corporations is a fine ideal but does not speak to the unparalleled strength and brutality of successful corporate efforts to keep workforces docile and unaware of their rights.

Five

THE LEGACY OF
COMPANY UNIONS

We never talk of workers' rights
I belong to the company-union;
They tell me that it leads to fights,
I belong to the company-union;
The company has always said
That men who talk like that are red,
We listen to the boss instead,
I belong to the company-union.[1]

When Washington Gladden advocated his profit-sharing plan in 1893, he could have easily been talking about the Saturn Corporation's "risk and reward" profit and productivity incentive plan a little more than a century later. His call for employers to share dividends is based on the belief that workers will then identify with their employers. In this way, the source for the strife between employers and employees would be eliminated. As discussed in chapter 2, Saturn does not have employees but "members." On the plant floor "op-techs" perform the work, not lineworkers. Hourly pay is called a salary and the reward is a share in the profits. Gladden had in mind workers who would be "partners and associates," not mere "hands." When Gladden urged that employers also enlist the eyes, brains, and hearts of workers, his comments were both retrospective and prospective. He hearkened back to a time in his own century when artisans were valued for their craft knowledge and not merely for their physical ability to repeat a task endlessly. He antici-pated our own time when many workers are valued for their knowledge

---

1. A worker's song about company unions. See Stuart D. Brandes, *American Welfare Capitalism: 1880–1940* (Chicago: University of Chicago Press, 1976), 119.

(however unacknowledged in their paycheck) and urged to get involved and participate to achieve ever greater productivity gains.

The concern that hovers over all programs that enlist the "whole worker" is the identity of the beneficiary. Is it true, as Gladden supposed, that not only managers, but workers benefit as well? For employee participation programs in our own day, do workers who participate in decision making that was once the sole province of management gain power, wages, and benefits that outweigh the difficulties of the additional work and stress that such programs engender? To help answer these questions, it is necessary to review the historical roots of employee participation programs in the United States. This entails a look at company unions, federal legislation in the 1930s and 1940s, the post–World War II business compact between labor and management, the TEAM Act, and recent rulings by the National Labor Relations Board on employee participation programs.

The issue of company unions or employer-sponsored representation plans versus independently organized trade unions is a vital historical question. It is a major theme in the history of organized labor in the first third of the twentieth century because it raises fundamental concerns about the way that power is understood and wielded in the workplace. Who decides what workers really want? Which employees are chosen to interpret workplace issues? How are they chosen? How much power do employee representatives have to address the demands of workers? These are not only issues for labor historians. They are also contemporary decisions facing workers who are involved in employee participation programs used by corporations across the country.

Company Unions

The definition of a "union" in the United States is not independent of the historical and legal framework in which it is situated. The definition that a union is simply a group of workers who band together for common goals and benefits is useful until one considers the role of the employer or management. The level of involvement employers and unions can have with each other's affairs is the point around which other issues revolve. The contested terrain between company unions and independently organized unions during the 1920s and 1930s is an important historical backdrop to contemporary discussions about the best way to represent the interests of workers.

A company union is an employer-supported group of workers who, in turn, negotiate with management concerning workplace conditions. Company unions are also known as employer-sponsored worker associations or nonunion employee representation plans.[2] Such formations can be traced back to "shop committees" organized as early as 1833 in the United States.[3] Since the passage of the National Labor Relations Act (NLRA) in 1935 and subsequent rulings by the National Labor Relations Board (NLRB), the meaning of a company union has been the subject of much litigation and deliberation. This will be discussed later in the chapter. But even before the NLRA's passage, the term "company union" had acquired a negative aura because such unions prevented organizing free of management and corporate interference.

The employee representation plan instituted at Straiton & Storm is a notable nineteenth-century example. In 1883, it was the largest cigar factory in the United States with over two thousand workers in its employ. In 1879, the company set up a board of arbitration, which had nine delegates, four elected by employees, four manager-appointed company representatives, and one other delegate chosen from a different branch of Straiton & Storm. Decisions were made by majority vote. The goal was to reduce adversarial relations between workers and management, ward off labor unrest and inculcate the idea that workers and employers had common interests.[4]

Another significant nineteenth-century company union was established in 1898 when William Filene's Sons in Boston set up the Filene Co-operative Association (FCA). The FCA maintained welfare funds for workers, which included medical and insurance plans. It also instituted a library and a bank. Social and athletic activities were sponsored by the Association.[5] By 1901, an arbitration board was formed with the authority to solve "cases of controversy" between the company and employees and also between employees. The philosophy of the FCA was grounded in the idea that employees' powers and responsibilities must

---

2. Bruce E. Kaufman, "Nonunion Employee Representation in the Pre-Wagner Act Years: A Reassessment," *Journal of Labor Research* 20, no. 1 (1999): 10.

3. Brandes, *American Welfare Capitalism*, 121.

4. Raymond L. Hogler and Guillermo J. Grenier, *Employee Participation and Labor Law in the American Workplace* (New York: Quorum Books, 1992), 14–15.

5. Daniel Nelson, "Employee Representation in Historical Perspective," in *Employee Representation: Alternatives and Future Directions*, ed. Bruce E. Kaufman and Morris M. Kleiner (Madison, Wisc.: Industrial Relations Research Association, 1993), 372.

be expanded so that they could "give their best to the business."[6] An account from 1915 claimed that the purpose of the FCA was to ensure that all employees had "sufficient voice in the store government . . . to make it just, considerate and effective."[7]

The motivations for starting company unions varied. Holbrook Fitz-john Porter, the vice president and general manager of the Nernst Lamp Company, founded a "factory committee" in 1903–4 for this electrical appliance manufacturer. His goal to institutionalize the "higher law in the industrial world" was prompted by his religious convictions. The committee was to be made up of workers, foremen, and clerical employees to help employees communicate concerns and offer suggestions to improve productivity.[8] C. W. Post had other purposes in mind for his cereal production plant in Battle Creek, Michigan. His company union, the National Trades and Worker Association (NTWA), was launched in 1910 to be a substitute for the American Federation of Labor (AFL) and independent union organizing. Unlike other unions, it would avoid strikes, boycotts, picketing, and coercion.[9]

Some company unions were modeled on the government of the United States. Workers could participate in this familiar environment and feel that just as they were involved in civic self-governance, so could they be involved in authentic self-governance in the workplace. John Leitch was a major figure at the Packard Piano Company in 1912, where he instituted regular plant-wide meetings and devised ways to compensate workers who developed techniques to save the corporation money. The workers elected a House of Representatives, and the Senate consisted of foremen appointees. The cabinet was made up of the executive officers, and the president, not surprisingly, was the president

6. Hogler and Grenier, Employee Participation, 16.

7. Nelson, "Employee Representation in Historical Perspective," 373. He refers to "A Thumbnail Sketch of the Filene Cooperative Association" (Boston, 1915). For more on Filene's, see Susan Porter Benson, Counter Cultures: Saleswomen, Managers, and Customers in American Department Stores, 1890–1940 (Urbana: University of Illinois Press, 1988). For an account of troublemakers at a Woolworth's five and dime store, see Dana Frank, "Girl Strikers Occupy Chain Store, Win Big: The Detroit Woolworth's Strike of 1937," in Howard Zinn, Dana Frank, and Robin D. G. Kelley, Three Strikes: Miners, Musicians, Salesgirls, and the Fighting Spirit of Labor's Last Century (Boston: Beacon Press, 2001), 57–118.

8. Brandes, American Welfare Capitalism, 122; Hogler and Grenier, Employee Participation, 16.

9. Nelson, "Employee Representation in Historical Perspective" 373.

of the company. The cabinet had veto power over "legislation" from the shop floor.[10]

John D. Rockefeller's company union at the Colorado Fuel & Iron Company is widely regarded as the most significant development in the history of late nineteenth- and early twentieth-century company unions.[11] The plan there was preceded by and prompted by a chilling episode in the history of labor in the United States. On April 20, 1914, when the Colorado militia stepped in and enforced the anti-union stance of Rockefeller's coal operators, the "Ludlow Massacre" was the result. The demands of the United Mine Workers of America for union recognition, wage increases, an eight-hour workday, freedom from compulsory purchases at the company store, and enforcement of Colorado mining laws were brutally suppressed. The union assembled a strike of twelve thousand miners among thirty-two nationalities, who set up a tent colony after being evicted from company housing. The militia set fire to the miners' colony and burned it to the ground, killing two women and eleven children. Three strike leaders were executed. From September 1913 to April 1914, sixty-six people from both sides of the conflict died.[12]

A national outcry resulted, and owner John D. Rockefeller was widely condemned for his complicity in these tragic events. After first instituting an aggressive public relations plan, Rockefeller's second strategy started with a letter to Mackenzie King, who was an expert in industrial relations and once the Canadian Secretary of Labor. Rockefeller accepted King's advice that capital and labor must engage in collective bargaining without, at the same time, going to the "extreme" of recognizing "unions of national and international character."[13] "Labor" was acceptable as long as laborers were not organized in unions developed independently of the Colorado Fuel & Iron Company.

Rockefeller instituted the Colorado Industrial Plan and announced it to his company officers and other employee representatives in October. The plan argued that unless "labor and capital join hands and recognize that their interest is a common interest, that what hurts one hurts the other, that what develops the well-being and prosperity of one must of

---

10. This summary of the Leitch Plan draws upon the work of Hogler and Grenier, *Employee Participation*, 17–18.

11. Kaufman, "Nonunion Employee Representation in the Pre-Wagner Act Years," 10.

12. Daniel Jacoby, *Laboring for Freedom: A New Look at the History of Labor in America* (Armonk, N.Y.: M. E. Sharpe, 1998), 94–95.

13. Hogler and Grenier, *Employee Participation*, 21.

necessity develop the well-being and prosperity of the other," then industrial peace and prosperity would be impossible.[14] The miners did vote for the plan although the United Mine Workers disputed the election. At one mine site the plan was voted down. Afterward, rumors spread that the mine would be shut down. Miners successfully petitioned for a new election in which the plan was easily voted in.[15]

The plan provided for local representation of the workers, though not on the basis of class or an independent union. Instead, industrial democracy was envisioned through joint committees of employee and management representatives. Workers did not have a say in wages or in other decisions previously reserved to management. The plan stated plainly that "officials of the company may decide any question without consulting committees or employees' representatives."[16] The significance of the Rockefeller Plan is that those in the steel industry and other industries used it as a model to avoid government interference in their firms during World War I. The plan was also used to counter union gains in both membership and economic clout that it achieved during the war.[17]

The next significant step in the evolution of employee representation plans occurred during the Wilson administration. The effort to preserve labor peace and industrial production during wartime prompted the creation of a War Labor Board (WLB) in 1918. This board consisted of five management members chosen by the National Industrial Conference Board, five labor representatives selected by the American Federation of Labor, and two representatives from the public chosen by both management and labor. The purpose was to settle controversies between management and labor that threatened production necessary for the war effort. The WLB also supported and promoted "shop committees" where independent unions did not exist to adjudicate differences. Some workers were not opposed to this idea since the committees could be an opening to worker control. By 1919, delegates to the convention of the American Federation of Labor argued that employee representation programs were "a delusion and a snare set up by the companies for the

14. Ibid., 27. They cite "To the People of Colorado," address to the Chamber of Commerce, Denver, Colorado, October 8, 1915, reprinted in John D. Rockefeller Jr., *The Personal Relation in Industry* (New York: Boni and Liveright, 1923).

15. Ibid., 28.

16. Ibid.

17. Ibid., 29.

express purpose of deluding the workers into the belief that they have some protection and thus have no need for trade union organization."[18]

The Rockefeller Plan and the work of the Wilson administration led to significant increases in the number of company-sponsored unions. In 1919, over 403,000 employees were plan members. By 1928, that number nearly quadrupled to over a million and a half employees. Company union membership constituted nearly 10 percent of all trade union members in 1919. This number reached 44.5 percent in 1928. In 1935, it rose to nearly 60 percent.[19]

The grave challenge that company unions posed to independent unions came clearly into focus in the steel industry. From the end of World War I until the mid-1930s, the U.S. steel industry engaged in vigorous efforts to thwart independent union organizing.[20] An early example is the Midvale Steel Company, which set up an employee representation plan in 1918 to respond to a union organization drive by the International Association of Machinists (IAM). Officials there relied on both the wording of Rockefeller's plan at the Colorado Fuel & Iron Company and the officials who implemented it to formulate their own plan at Midvale. Elected representatives of the steelworkers voted unanimously for the plan despite the objections of the IAM, which argued that the workers were forced into the decision. During a hearing set up by the War Labor Board (WLB), the vice president of Midvale admitted that the plan was designed to accomplish its goal "without dealing with organized labor."[21] The second example is the Bethlehem Steel Company, also in 1918. The complaints of machinists and electrical workers at the main plant in Bethlehem prompted the WLB to rule that the problems there were detrimental to the war effort. The WLB determined that employees had no means of collective bargaining and lacked a direct voice in determining working conditions. Bethlehem not only recruited Midvale's vice president to help set up its plan, but it also sought out two officials from Colorado Fuel & Iron. The goal was to circumvent the WLB's findings and to take advantage of the fact that the WLB did not require Bethle-

---

18. Ibid., 34. They cite *Report of Proceedings of the Thirty-ninth Annual Convention of the American Federation of Labor* (Washington, D.C.: Law Reporter Printing Co., 1919), 249–50.

19. Ibid., 35.

20. Ibid.

21. Ibid., 38.

hem Steel to recognize the IAM. As a result, the company was free to set up a company union.[22]

The Midvale and Bethlehem plans thus initiated a trend that culminated with 90 percent of all steelworkers belonging to a company union by the end of 1934. Not content with the steel industry alone, the National Association of Manufacturers and the American Management Association both contributed funds and sponsored events to promote employee representation plans in other companies. The idea that company unions were being organized to thwart independent organizing was substantiated by a telling statistic released in 1935 by the Bureau of Labor Statistics. Of the employers surveyed, nearly 42 percent responded that they put together employee representation plans to ward off independent trade union organizing.[23]

Legislative Responses to Company Unions

A significant legislative response to company unions occurred on June 16, 1933, when President Franklin D. Roosevelt signed the National Industrial Recovery Act (NIRA). The key section of this legislation was Section 7(a), which provided employees with the right to "organize and bargain collectively through representatives of their own choosing" without employer coercion. Employees would neither be forced to join a company union nor prevented from joining any other labor organization of their choice. According to one assessment of the NIRA, workers who were taught that unions were un-American in the 1920s could now see unions as a step for national economic recovery in the middle of the Depression years.[24]

The steel industry took advantage of the vagueness of the NIRA to argue that their employer-sponsored unions were in keeping with the intent of the legislation. Weirton Steel was at the center of this successful effort. Six days after the enactment of the NIRA, Weirton introduced an employee representation plan based on the Bethlehem Plan. The vote that occurred afterward was not whether to accept the plan but for the representatives who would serve on the Weirton Steel Employees' Representation Plan. Nearly 85 percent of Weirton's employees voted and

---

22. Ibid., 38–39.

23. Ibid., 41.

24. John Hennen, "E. T. Weir, Employee Representation, and the Dimensions of Social Control: Weirton Steel, 1933–1937," *Labor Studies Journal* 26, no. 3 (2001): 25–26.

they selected forty-nine representatives. In response, the Amalgamated Association of Iron, Steel, and Tin Workers kicked off an organizing drive in July in opposition. Strikes broke out at three different locations of the Weirton operation, and strikers demanded recognition of the union. The strikers had a determined opponent in the founder of the company, Ernest Weir. He argued that Weirton already had a union through the company plan presented to and voted on by the employees. He insisted he would deal only with the representatives of that plan. Weir refused to recognize Amalgamated and reopened the closed mills. In October, the union appealed to the newly formed National Labor Board (formed in August 1933 by authorization of President Roosevelt and chaired by Senator Robert Wagner). A compromise to hold a new election resulted in the employees voting, once again on December 11, for the company plan. The NLB was not allowed to monitor the election and the board charged that Weirton coerced the employees with firings, threats of discharge and plant closures, and gifts and additional compensation to employee representatives. The government decided to press forward with a suit against Weirton in view of Section 7(a) of the NIRA. The government's attempt to charge Weirton Steel that it had violated the NIRA by starting its own union did not succeed. Narrowly considered, the court did not accept the government's evidence of voting irregularities. Nor did the court accept the charge that the Weirton plan kept workers from seeking recourse for their grievances. Still larger clouds loomed over proponents of independent unions. The vagueness of the NIRA on the meaning of collective bargaining, who was legally empowered to undertake such bargaining, and the NLB's lack of enforcement power over employers remained unresolved issues.[25]

A close study of the rise and durability of company unions in the first third of the twentieth century is eye-opening. Big steel, the behemoth of American industry at that time, had a chokehold on the union movement. Independent unions were not available without massive struggle. The ability of the industry to simultaneously set up company unions and resist government oversight was remarkable in its scope and success. Weirton Steel is the most striking example because even with legislation and direct governmental oversight through the NLB, Weirton still prevailed. Plainly stated, the very definition of a union was still up for debate. Until this could be answered, the struggle among independent

25. Hogler and Grenier, Employee Participation, 43–48.

unions, corporations, and their company unions as well as the labor board of the federal government would remain unfinished.

The significance of the contemporary fact that a union, by definition, is independent and separate from its company must not be underestimated. Yet such an assumption could not be made before the passage of the National Labor Relations Act in 1935. Only the determined struggle of union organizers coupled with favorable federal legislation was able to turn back determined and resourceful corporations that wanted to maintain control over their workers.

The defeat of effective federal oversight over company unions at Weirton Steel did not deter continued efforts. Senator Robert Wagner tried again in 1934 with the Labor Disputes Bill, which he withdrew only months after he introduced it. In 1935, he introduced the National Labor Relations Act (NLRA), or the Wagner Act, which Roosevelt signed into law that July. The NLRA is a voluminous piece of federal legislation. Section 7 in the NLRA on the formation of unions and the prohibition of company unions is particularly pertinent.

> Employees shall have the right to self-organization, to form, join, or assist labor organizations, to bargain through representatives of their own choosing, and to engage in other concerted activities for the purpose of collective bargaining or other mutual aid or protection, and shall also have the right to refrain from any or all such activities.[26]

Standing alone, Section 7 would not be an advance over the regulations of the National Industrial Recovery Act. Without additional clarification, the definition and practice of "self-organization," "labor organization," and bargaining with "representatives of one's own choosing" could easily be functional equivalents of what occurred in the company unions. But Section 8 of the NLRA defines "unfair labor practices," pertaining to both employers and unions. For instance, Section 8(a)(1) says that it is an unfair labor practice for employers "to interfere with, restrain, or coerce employees in the exercise of the rights guaranteed in section 7."[27] Section 8(a)(2) further stipulates that it is an unfair

---

26. See the National Labor Relations Act, Section 7, in Michael Yates, *Power on the Job: The Legal Rights of Working People* (Boston: South End Press, 1994), 76. His useful book provides an explanation of the significance of various aspects of the NLRA.

27. Yates, *Power on the Job*, 80.

labor practice for an employer "to dominate or interfere with the formation or administration of any labor organization or contribute financial support to it."[28] This part of Section 8 effectively rules out company unions. A union must not be of the company's choosing but the workers' "own choosing." Otherwise the activity of a company constitutes domination or interference. Existing company unions were ruled illegal and the formation of new ones prohibited.

World War II and the Postwar Business Compact

The period of World War II itself has been underestimated in labor history as a formative time that would affect postwar labor law and labor relations. Such is the judgment of one historian who argues that policies during the war that focused on increased and continuous production ensured the stability of labor relations, and restricted the scope of militancy among rank-and-file workers would continue to hold sway after the war.[29] For example, in 1944 the United Auto Workers adopted a policy that shifted control of the union away from its constituent locals to the international level. Employees who wished to go on strike without proper authorization would be disciplined or the local itself would be subject to intervention or replacement by the international. Thus, the phenomenon usually associated with the period after World War II, namely, that employees should present grievances through the union administrative structure rather than exercising their own direct action against the employer, emerged during the war itself. This perspective shows that the roots of the postwar business compact are much deeper than usually supposed.[30]

The rise of organized labor during and after World War II is a major aspect of the mid-century American economic order. Membership in unions jumped from 8.9 million in 1940 to 14.9 million in 1946. At the end of World War II, 35.5 percent of the civilian labor force belonged to unions. Most of the basic industries had union organization rates of 80 percent to 100 percent.[31] Such organization led to successful strikes

---

28. Ibid.

29. James B. Atleson, *Labor and the Wartime State: Labor Relations and Law during World War II* (Urbana: University of Illinois Press, 1998), 1–2.

30. Ibid., 149.

31. Kim Moody, *An Injury to All: The Decline of American Unionism* (London and New York: Verso, 1988), 17.

against major industrial employers that pushed for wage cutbacks. While union activity during and especially after World War II may be considered "militant" by current standards, the prevailing philosophy of most unions at that time emphasized that the labor movement existed primarily to enhance the economic living standards of its members. This type of unionism is called business unionism.

> Business unionism was of course not new in the 1950s. Most AFL unions had practiced it for decades. The growth of business union-ism began when most of the top leaders of the AFL repudiated socialism before the turn of the century. In 1890, AFL President Samuel Gompers declared: "The trade unions pure and simple are the natural organizations of the wageworkers to secure their present material and practical improvement and to achieve their final emancipation." Adolph Strasser, another early AFL leader and friend of Gompers, said, "We have no ultimate ends. We are going on from day to day. We are fighting for immediate objects — objects that can be realized in a few years."[32]

The pacts forged between labor and capital during and just after World War II completed a process of redefining worker agitation to fit the accepted boundaries of dissent within capitalism. The Taft-Hartley Act of 1947 codified these parameters by banning sympathy strikes and secondary boycotts. Unions could strike only against their own employer and not in support of other unions. The use of boycotts against related companies was deemed illegal. The Taft-Hartley Act represented a major blow to the hopes raised by the National Labor Relations Act passed twelve years earlier.

The passage of Taft-Hartley was not an immediate death knell for unionism in the United States, as its provisions were not always followed. Only recently have replacement workers been called in regularly to break strikes. This anti-union weapon was not utilized widely until Ronald Reagan set a precedent by calling in workers to stop the Professional Air Traffic Controllers (PATCO) strike in 1981. In the relatively pro-labor years that followed World War II, labor was able to consolidate its hard-won gains for which it had struggled since the 1930s. The "traditional Workplace Contract" is one way to describe how labor accomplished

---

32. Ibid., 55–56.

these goals.[33] The negotiations and tradeoffs that labor made with capital just after World War II go to the heart of business unionism. While labor won steadily increasing wages, benefits, and job security during the "glory years" from 1947 to 1973, they gave up "meaningful input into the strategic decisions of the firm beyond the workplace per se. Thus the Workplace Contract provided labor with a measure of control over wages, but not corporate investment; over who was laid off, but not over who was hired; over working conditions in a factory or mine, but not over the nature, the prices, or the quality of the product or service produced."[34]

A typical labor agreement or "Workplace Contract" covers, at least, seven points. These include cost-of-living adjustments and annual wage increases; collectively bargained "fringe" benefits; seniority-based layoffs, recalls, transfers, and promotions; negotiated work rules, job descriptions, and classifications; grievance machinery to resolve disputes over contract interpretation; on-site union representation and a union security provision that ensures, except where prohibited, that all workers at a unionized site belong to the union. The last provision of the Workplace Contract relates to management rights. This provision is most important because it "assures that management will retain the decision-making authority over all issues not explicitly delineated in the contract."[35] Labor and management, through the collective bargaining process, negotiate issues that are directly pertinent to the workplace. The typical management-rights clause pertains to matters relating to the overall enterprise. This includes the following: control over design and engineering of the product or service; the methods, means, and processes of manufacture or provision of a service; all pricing decisions; the determination of quality standards; control over subcontracting and production location decisions; determination of all financing and investment activity; unilateral control over decisions bearing on where to locate and when to expand production and when and under what circumstances to close down all or part of an operation.[36]

---

33. See Barry Bluestone and Irving Bluestone, *Negotiating the Future: A Labor Perspective on American Business* (New York: Basic Books, 1992), esp. chapter 2, "The Glory Days and the Traditional Workplace Contract," 33–59.

34. Ibid., 43.

35. Ibid., 51.

36. Ibid., 52.

The battle over such management rights was basically finished by the end of the 1940s. The five-year contract negotiated between the United Auto Workers and General Motors in 1950 typified the post-war Workplace Contract. *Fortune* magazine called it the "treaty of Detroit" and hailed GM's gain of control over "crucial management functions." As such, it could plan its labor relations with confidence. No U.S. manufacturer in the United States had been able to do this for years.[37]

Employee Participation Programs

The emergence of employee participation plans and labor-management cooperation programs in the American workplace occurred in the early 1970s. This new phase of employee representation in this century marked a departure from an overtly hierarchical and top-down management style. Instead, workers were invited to speak up, get involved, and volunteer ideas for the good of the entire business. The overall objective was to motivate workers by instilling in them the idea that they were no longer cogs in the corporate machine. Rather, workers are valued members of a common enterprise. One common example of such practices includes naming retail clerks "partners" or "associates." The idea, on a rhetorical level, is to narrow the gap between "workers" and "owners."

Industrialists in the United States initiated participation programs to respond to successful Japanese and European challenges to U.S. supremacy in product quality and worker productivity. The automobile industry was the first in the United States to adopt these programs. Mike Parker and Jane Slaughter, in *Working Smart: A Union Guide to Participation Programs and Reengineering*, define participation programs in this way:

> [They] involve special events away from the job: meetings of quality circles, task forces, joint labor-management committees. . . . These circles brainstorm ideas about productivity, quality, and/or working conditions, and almost always include both workers and members of management. The cooperation apparatus includes new positions such as full-time facilitators and trainers. It involves a

---

37. Ibid., 54. I am indebted to the Bluestones for this description and summary of the traditional workplace contract.

new set of management policies, including particular definitions of "quality," "competitiveness," the "needs of the customer," and worker participation and dignity.[38]

In the late 1970s, management introduced "Quality of Work Life" programs to respond to studies and anecdotal evidence that blue-collar work was "numbing down" American workers, which led to unproductive workers and shoddy production. The goal included the improvement in working conditions. By the early 1980s, "Employee Improvement" and "Employee Participation" were buzzwords in which workers were urged to think of themselves as more integral to the entire work process. Rather than only angling for improvements in working conditions, workers should think of themselves as "associates" who are part of an overall team effort to achieve common objectives. The "Team Concept" caught hold in the latter part of the 1980s in the auto industry. In the steel industry, "Labor-Management Participation Teams" were instituted. At Xerox, "Commodity Study Teams" were implemented. In the 1990s, Total Quality Management (TQM) techniques reemphasized the overall objectives of a corporation in order to coordinate workers' individual efforts. "The emphasis was on top management setting the course; 'strong leadership' became the rage again, rather than the softer consensus style of the 1980s."[39] Finally, "reengineering" and "reinventing" move beyond TQM and ask about the relevance of entire work procedures rather than tinkering with quality improvements in already existing programs.[40]

The legal status of employee programs has always been in question and has been the subject of much legal maneuvering. In a unionized setting, all participation programs are illegal if the union does not approve their use. In addition, there are some types of participation programs that even a union cannot approve. An employer under Section 8(a)(2) may not "dominate or assist" a team, circle, task force, or any participation group that is a labor organization. The proliferation of such programs, the range of the industries in which they can be found, and the extent to

---

38. Mike Parker and Jane Slaughter, *Working Smart: A Union Guide to Participation Programs and Reengineering* (Detroit: Labor Notes, 1994), 1.

39. Ibid., 3.

40. This historical sketch is a summary of Chapter 1 of *Working Smart: A Union Guide to Participation Programs and Reengineering*, entitled "From QWL to Reengineering: How We Got Here" (1–8).

which they are applied in any given company cannot be confused with the actual legality of their use.[41]

In 1992, employee participation programs caught the attention of the Clinton administration. During his first campaign for the presidency and in the early years of his first term, Bill Clinton sought to position himself somewhere between unfettered capitalism and the supposedly discredited economics of the welfare state. This turned out to be an American version of the "third-way" in economic theorizing that Tony Blair of Britain and Gerhard Schröder of Germany also sought to implement. In one way, Clinton himself made a connection between covenantal ideas and participation programs. On the cover copy for the paperback edition of Barry Bluestone and Irving Bluestone's *Negotiating the Future: A Labor Perspective on American Business*, Clinton's endorsement reads as follows: "The Bluestones offer a New Covenant for labor and management based on participation, cooperation, and teamwork. Such an approach to working smarter will have to be adopted if America is to regain its competitive edge." In remarks before the Hillsborough County Retired Teachers Association on March 6, 1992, Clinton opined that "a General Motors plant in Texas is saving the jobs because the workers said no to the bosses of their own union. And they said, 'We are going to scrap these work rules. We are going to be flexible. We are going to save our jobs by having the courage to change.' And that's what we are all going to have to do."[42]

Catching the spirit of teamwork, flexibility, and participation, the Clinton administration appointed the Commission on the Future of Worker-Management Relations, a joint effort of the Commerce and Labor Departments. Known also as the Dunlop Commission (after John Dunlop, a former secretary of labor), its main objective was to envision a new future for the role of labor and management. The commission had three tasks. The first was a review of possible methods or institutions to enhance productivity through labor-management cooperation and employee participation. The second point concerned changes to the present legal framework and practices of collective bargaining to enhance cooperative behavior, improve productivity, and reduce conflict and delay.

---

41. For concerns about the legal status of Saturn's "co-management," see Saul A. Rubinstein and Thomas A. Kochan, *Learning from Saturn: Possibilities for Corporate Governance and Employee Relations* (Ithaca, N.Y.: ILR Press, 2001), 137–39.

42. Parker and Slaughter, *Working Smart*, 7.

The third point focused on ways to help those involved in workplace problems to resolve these issues directly rather than through recourse to state or federal courts or other governmental bodies.[43]

The Dunlop Commission was composed of academics and labor and business leaders. It concluded that the workplace should be open "to a variety of new experiments with employee participation and labor-management partnerships and bring the benefits of these innovations to more workers and workplaces."[44] After seventeen national and regional hearings, the commission argued that "employee participation and labor-management partnerships are good for workers, firms, and the national economy."[45] The significance of the Dunlop Commission is threefold. One, it put a stamp of approval on thousands of then existing participation programs which, depending on one's definition of a participation program, included between one-fifth and one-third of the total U.S. workforce. Two, it called for a clarification on regulations in the National Labor Relations Act (NLRA) that have been interpreted as severely restricting the scope and application of participation programs, if not prohibiting them altogether. Overall, it provided a set of ideas to support Clinton's attempt to make U.S. workers flexible and internationally competitive while simultaneously preserving protection for them in the new globalized economy.

The employer concern that employee participation programs were vulnerable to successful legal challenges was well-founded. Employers and employer organizations interested in setting up such programs suffered a significant setback when the National Labor Relations Board in 1992 ruled in favor of the employees in *Electromation v. Teamsters Local 1049*. When workers spoke up against wages and working conditions at Electromation, Inc., a nonunion company in Elkhart, Indiana, the company attempted to set up five "action committees." At this point, the Teamsters decided to commence an organizing drive among workers at Electromation. Electromation then suspended the committees, which it said it would restart if the unionizing drive failed — and it did fail. Employees charged that this constituted unfair manipulation of the election. The Teamsters then filed a suit on behalf of the workers

---

43. Commission on the Future of Worker-Management Relations, *Report and Recommendations* (Washington, D.C.: GPO, 1994), xvi.
44. Ibid., xvii.
45. Ibid.

at Electromation to abolish the action committees and to hold another election.

Even the National Labor Relations Board, whose membership was composed entirely of members appointed by the Reagan and Bush administrations (1980–92), ruled in favor of the union. The Seventh Circuit Court of Appeals upheld the NLRB decision. It argued that "Electromation actually controlled which issues received attention by the committee and which did not. It unilaterally determined how many could serve on each committee . . . and . . . which committees certain employees would serve on, thus exercising significant control over the employee's participation and voice."[46] Conveniently, management had already reserved to itself membership on the action committees, which assured that they would be a presence on the labor side of the table when the action committees met with management. Not only did Electromation lose its case in the courts, but it also lost on the shop floor as the Teamsters ran a second election (after the NLRB ruling) and won. The *Electromation* decision vindicated the intent of Section 8(a)(2) of the National Labor Relations Act because it showed that management was trying to dominate the committee that would supposedly represent the workers' interest. "This was real empowerment, for the employees went on to form a union under their own control and used it to win an enforceable contract with their employer."[47]

The Dunlop Commission did not give rise to any fundamental changes in U.S. labor law. As such, organized labor and the business sector were not satisfied ultimately with its recommendations. It did highlight two issues. One, it alerted already existing employer-sponsored programs to involve employees in workplace decision making on production and quality issues. Second, it focused attention on the deficiencies of the National Labor Relations Act. Business interests sought more flexibility to negotiate with workers outside of the union structure as it has been defined since 1935. As for labor, it sought more serious efforts to amend federal labor law to create a favorable legal atmosphere for organizing and holding corporations accountable for disrupting union activity.

---

46. This summary of the Electromation decision comes from James R. Rundle and Patricia A. Greenfield, "Worker Representation without Worker Consent," *WorkingUSA* (July/August 1997): 65.

47. Ibid.

The TEAM Act

The persistence of corporate attempts to dilute or deny worker representation in the workplace is remarkable. The National Association of Manufacturers (NAM) contributed funds in the 1930s to support employee representation plans. In the 1990s as well, they advocated the passage of new legislation to weaken the core provisions of federal labor law. The U.S. Chamber of Commerce and the Labor Policy Association were also involved in promoting the TEAM Act as a direct result of not achieving their goals through the Dunlop Commission. In short, the TEAM Act, or Teamwork for Employees and Managers Act, was aimed at negating the core rationale for the NLRA — the prohibition of company unions or employer-sponsored representation plans. The central provision of the act was amendment by addition to Section 8(a)(2). In nonunion settings, the TEAM Act would allow teams of employees to discuss the terms and conditions of their employment. In union settings, its proponents argued that the TEAM Act would not interfere with the existing bargaining unit. Under the House bill that passed 221–202 on September 27, 1995, employers would be able to:

> establish, assist, maintain, or participate in any organization or entity of any kind, in which employees participate to at least the same extent practicable as representatives of management participate, to address matters of mutual interest, including, but not limited to, issues of quality, productivity, efficiency, and safety and health.[48]

In a statement released on February 22, 1995, the AFL-CIO noted that the TEAM Act would allow employers to create, fund, and deal with a rival, company-controlled entity — even for those companies that already have a union. "What this bill ultimately is about, then, is not teamwork but control. Management seeks what it has always sought: the freedom to 'involve' employees in ways that do not threaten management prerogatives. The ultimate goal is what it always has been: to stifle legitimate worker voice and to stave off genuine worker participation."[49] Clinton vetoed this legislation in July 1996. The bill was reintroduced in February of 1997. In words that echoed his pro-business colleagues of the 1930s, then Rep. Harris Fawell (R.) of Illinois declared

---

48. This is the language from the U.S. Senate bill. Congress, Senate, *Teamwork for Employees and Managers Act of 1997*, 105th Cong., 1st sess., S. 295.

49. *www.aflcio.org.*

to his colleagues on the House floor that TEAM would "remove road-blocks in current law to workplace cooperation and increased employee involvement, while *not* undermining the ability of workers to choose union representation."[50] Fawell proclaimed that the workplace alterna-tive without the passage of the TEAM Act would be a return to the "just work, don't think," top-down management of yesteryear.[51] In com-plete disregard of labor history and the scourge of company unions in the earlier part of the century, Fawell then remarked: "My sense is that the TEAM Act deals with a hybrid form of workplace organization that may not have been considered when our labor law was written many decades ago."[52] It was exactly because of such hybrid organizations and the deleterious effects they had on independent worker organizing that the National Labor Relations Act was written.

Company Unions at an Aluminum Can Factory?

The TEAM Act did not get a floor vote during the 105th Congress. Yet the business sector remained active in other ways. The Labor Policy Association (LPA), based in Washington, D.C., continued to promote al-ternatives despite the setbacks suffered with the *Electromation* decision, the Dunlop Commission, and the TEAM Act. As their self-adulatory website notes, the LPA is a "highly respected voice advocating the interests of human resource executives in the public policy arena."[53] According to their mission statement, the LPA is a "public policy advo-cacy organization representing corporate executives interested in human resource policy from more than 200 leading organizations doing business in the United States."[54] Their purpose is to provide the information, analysis, and opinion to their members to influence emerging trends in labor and employment policy so that they can "achieve [their] strategic human resource objectives."[55] LPA member companies in the United States employ thirteen million workers, or more than 12 percent of the private-sector workforce.

---

50. The Honorable Harris W. Fawell, *Extension of Remarks, Introduction of the Teamwork for Employees and Managers (TEAM) Act*, February 6, 1997.

51. Ibid.

52. Ibid.

53. *www.lpa.org.*

54. Ibid.

55. Ibid.

An important example of their work occurred in 2001 when the LPA filed an *amicus curiae* brief to the National Labor Relations Board (NLRB) for Crown Cork & Seal Co., an aluminum can manufacturing plant in Sugar Land, Texas, with 150 employees. A regional director of the NLRB filed a charge against the company on the basis that the work teams at Crown were really company-dominated labor organizations that dealt with employees concerning work conditions in violation of Section 8(a)(2) of the NLRA. The work teams at Crown consisted of four production teams composed solely of production workers. In addition, three oversight teams composed of workers and management dealt with safety issues, layoff procedures, and all terms and conditions of employment. On July 20, 2001, in a unanimous decision that cited the LPA's brief, the NLRB ruled that Crown's employee involvement program was legal. According to the LPA, the ruling is so significant that the need for the TEAM Act is now moot and the legal issues surrounding the "sophisticated employee involvement structures" prevalent throughout American industry are "once and for all" resolved.

This decision did not get the fanfare that surrounded the TEAM Act and is a significant example of the determination to chip away at the protections that the NLRA provides. In sum, the ruling centered on the words "dealing with" found in Section 2(5) of the NLRA.[56] A labor organization (such as a union) "deals with" employers concerning grievances, labor disputes, wages, rates of pay, hours of employment, or conditions of work. An unfair labor practice is when a company dominates or supports an organization which undertakes such tasks. Citing past rulings, the board agreed that the work teams and committees at Crown are not true labor organizations because they "perform essentially managerial functions." Therefore, they cannot be said to "deal with" management. In a direct quote from the LPA's brief, the NLRB ruling declared that "within their delegated spheres of authority, the seven committees *are* management."[57]

The contention that the production workers at Crown Cork are management is astounding. The regional NLRB argued that the work committees do not possess authority that is "final and absolute."[58] Thus, by definition the seven committees necessarily had to be "dealing" with

---

56. Crown Cork & Seal Company Inc. and Martin Rodriguez (334 NLRB No. 92. Case No. 16-CA-18316. July 20, 2001). Amended July 31, 2001.

57. Ibid.

58. Ibid.

management when their recommendations are passed on to the plant manager for final approval. This argument was rejected on the grounds that rarely are any managerial decisions final and absolute in any plant. Rather than "dealing with," what occurs at Crown is the "familiar process of a managerial recommendation making its way up the chain of command."[59] The contention that workers are, in fact, managers was assumed throughout the decision. It is the premise that supports the claim that existing labor law had nothing to do with the events at Crown.

The significance of this ruling is that a precedent has been set to continue the watering down of the National Labor Relations Act. The litigation to find and exploit legal loopholes that step around the spirit and intent of the Act will continue. The imaginative process that accords managerial status to aluminum can workers in Sugar Land, Texas, is admirable for its boldness and unabashed twisting of a simple truth. The owners or plant manager of Crown Cork & Seal may decide to move the company across the border to Mexico, slash wages, or eliminate the production teams. Or they may decide unilaterally on any number of ways to make life miserable for the workers there. No matter what status the LPA or the NLRB accords the workers, there is absolutely nothing the "managers" can do to stop the onslaught.

To be sure, the ruling at Crown does not preclude the formation of a union. But the secure legal status of the work committees at Crown makes it far more difficult for a union organizing effort to gain traction on the issues in which "work committees" of production workers and managers are already cooperating. Such cooperation is co-optation, and it is one more way for workers to lose an independent voice in the workplace. This has been the intent of company unions throughout their history. In Crown, and in literally thousands of corporations around the country, this is posed as a workers' rights issue. It is claimed, rightly, that workers want a say in their daily work life. But is employee input couched within structures that management designs or do workers have their own chance to design their own means of expression and, if need be, opposition? The decision at Crown is not one that orients workers toward self-determination in the workplace. It does not absolutely preclude self-determination, but it creates an atmosphere in which such efforts are greatly hindered.

---

59. Ibid.

Conclusion

On the surface, cooperation in the workplace through an employee participation program seems to partake of great moral wisdom. Is it not true that cooperation is the way to put into practice the Christian ideals of justice and love? As an abstract moral ideal, it seems to be nearly impervious to abstract moral criticism. But an ethic that rests content with abstract or, worse yet, transcendental or "revealed" moral ideals is for those who prefer mystification over explanation. Moral norms are not transcendental in character and not independent of the historical contexts from which they arise. Thus a consideration of the public policy implications of any theological and moral claim is especially warranted. Covenantal business ethics fail on this point because they do not account for the legal consequences of their moral and theological claims. Christian covenantal business ethics must account for the legal limits that corporate management must observe when enlisting workers onto the "team." Covenantal business ethicists try to move beyond "mere contractualism." Thus, it is understandable why discussions of legal precedents do not loom large in their work. What is "right" cannot be delimited by what is "merely legal." Yet to consider the point of what is "legal" is to gain insight on the possible practical standing of one's claim about what is "right" or "morally good." Not all workplaces are unionized, but the failure of many advocates of Christian covenantal ethics to consider their claims in the context of a unionized workplace is an avoidable limitation of their work.[60] Their neglect of the legal aspects of happenings on the shop-floor is coupled with the failure to see that the implementation of a covenantal ethic along the lines proposed by enthusiasts of employee participation programs would seriously compromise the integrity of a labor union's mission.

Among many advocates of a covenantal ethic, there is little said about the union's role in protecting workers' rights. A "covenantal" relationship is privileged over relationships forged on a "contractual" basis because covenants, it is argued, partake of a higher morality as they are rooted in caring and love and acts of supererogation. The problem with such a morality as it pertains to labor-management relations is the extraordinary difficulty management already has in living up to its contractual duties. To privilege covenantal relationships in the workplace is

---

60. Stewart Herman's *Durable Goods: A Covenantal Ethic for Management and Employees* (discussed in chapter 2) is an exception on this point.

the first step of a dangerous journey. This peril arises from the assumption that covenantal norms are appropriate to relationships predicated on and determined by vast differences in power and material resources. It is said that the devil is in the details. It is exactly in the details that a union may bedevil the capacity of management to act unjustly and with impunity at any moment. The details, forged on the hard anvil of giving and taking at the negotiating table, are vitally important to workers who depend or will come to depend upon them for survival.

Contemporary employee participation programs promote the idea that workers and management are "in the same boat together" when, in fact, they are not. Implicit to the "same boat" rhetoric is that both parties are subject to the same choppy waters and the same miserable weather. This is simply not true. Participation programs mystify capital and management's superior position by according surface decision-making power to workers. At the same time, they leave the basic structure of ownership and management firmly in place. Protections accorded to management do not extend to workers when rainy days arrive. The application of "covenantal" or "cooperative" norms to the workplace also fails to account for the ways that management can take advantage of its superior power to force concessions on workers who would otherwise not accept them under a more "adversarial" labor relations stance. Such programs work counter to the idea of trade unionism — the "we-they" concept. "Solidarity means *we* stick together against *them*."[61] Participation programs fail to see the contradictory interests of management and workers. Management has the task of maximizing profits and the union must ensure a better life for its workers. The long-term interests of management and workers are in conflict, and this conflict is fundamental and primary.[62]

The neglect of the contractual aspect of workplace relationships in covenantal business ethics indicates an unacceptable and disturbing nonchalance toward the imbalance of power and privilege between labor and capital that contracts are intended to redress. This is really the core problem with the proposals pertaining to cooperation between labor and management. Such proposals assume that partnerships can exist because there is equality between the parties, when, in fact, there is not. This is particularly insidious because even in those workplaces where there

---

61. Parker and Slaughter, *Working Smart*, 131.
62. Ibid., 146–47.

are unions, management always insists on dealing with workers as individuals or teams of individuals in the employee participation programs. Workers are never approached as members of a union. In the name of flexibility in the workplace and national and international competitiveness, union members are asked to go along with new managerial regimes without specifically referring to or revisiting the union contract. To urge on workers a covenantal ethic that places the emphasis on cooperation only aids and abets forces in business that see corporate viability and the elimination of "cumbersome work rules" and "old-school" style unionism as complementary. Covenantal ethics do not address these important issues.

Six

A "PROTESTING" LABOR ETHIC AT WORK

=====================================

Remember who you are. Remember where you come from. Change
the world. — Ralph Fasanella[1]

The statistics for organized labor are not encouraging. Unionized workers comprise only 9 percent of the private sector labor force and 13.5 percent overall if the public sector is included. Nearly one hundred million workers are not organized. How one relates to those who own or control the workplace is a daily issue in the United States. There is little doubt about the extraordinary difficulty of organizing in the manufacturing sector, given the ability of corporations to move factory operations, nearly at will, around the world. In 1999, it looked like a turnaround was in the making as there was a net gain of 265,000 union members across the nation. Such success in union organizing had not been experienced since the late 1970s. But in 2000, union density levels dropped again, according to a government report.[2] Another measure of the activity of organized labor is the use of the strike. One might point to the extraordinary success of the Teamsters strike in 1997 against the United Parcel Service. This undoubted success still does not compare to the activity and struggles of the nineteenth century and the strikes during and after World War I and World War II. For instance, in 1945–46 almost all of the major industrial unions went on strike for wage increases. In 1946, 4.5 million workers went on 4,600 strikes. In the next eleven years, an average of 370 major strikes (for work sites with at least one thousand

---

1. Ralph Fasanella, "A Self-Taught Artist's Blue-Collar City and What's Left of It," *New York Times*, March 24, 2002, sec. 14, p. 5.
2. Kate Bronfenbrenner, "'Changing to Organize': Unions Know What Has to Be Done. Now They Have to Do It," *The Nation* 3, no. 10 (September 2001): 16.

workers) occurred each year involving more than 1.5 million workers each year.[3]

From car builders in Spring Hill to can producers in Sugar Land, workers across the nation confront a job landscape that is markedly different from that of their parents or grandparents. It is amazing that workers once stopped trains coast to coast and even took over the governance of a major U.S. city for a spell in 1877. When the mild John J. Sweeney assumed the presidency of the AFL-CIO in 1995 and merely suggested something about "blocking a bridge," howls from the business community were heard from coast to coast. The fact that workers once demanded, not asked, to be treated as human beings is what some Saturn workers remember fondly about the "old world." The new world, complete now with its own theo-covenantal justifications, beckons and seduces workers toward its paradigm of cooperation. The shift is nearly complete. Among corporations with five thousand or more employees, 96 percent have some sort of employee involvement program.[4] As corporations consider the "labor question" in their boardrooms, there could be no better news than this. According to major indices of economic well-being in the workplace — wages, pensions, length of hours spent at work, health care benefits, and workplace safety issues — workers in the United States are worse off today than they were twenty years ago *before* the widespread introduction of employee participation programs. One may argue that other factors account for the decline of workers' prospects. Yet it is hard to imagine how continued accommodation to management enthusiasm for "team spirit" is going to reverse this situation. Odd how certain members of the same team are more equal than others. In 1965, CEOs in major companies earned 20.3 times more than an average worker. This ratio rocketed to 106.9 times the wage of an average worker in 1999. In that year, a CEO needed to work only for half a week to earn the same amount that an average worker earned in fifty-two weeks.[5] Corporations have been waging a successful class war for some time, and laborers are not on the winning side.

---

3. Barry Bluestone and Irving Bluestone, *Negotiating the Future: A Labor Perspective on American Business* (New York: Basic Books, 1992), 41, n. 38, 271, and Moody, *An Injury to All*, 18.

4. "The Team Act," Labor Policy Association, *www.lpa.org*.

5. The earnings ratio of CEOs to workers was 28.5 in 1978 and 55.9 in 1989. Lawrence Mishel, Jared Bernstein, and John Schmitt, *The State of Working America, 2000/2001* (Ithaca, N.Y.: ILR Press, 2001), 211.

A Shift in Ethics from Business to Labor

Business ethics is a well-established field, and Protestant Christian ethicists have been generous contributors to the study of the norms and principles that are to guide the practices of companies and their leaders. But from the savings and loan debacle of the 1980s to the Enron scandal in the first decade of the twenty-first century, it has been difficult to say the words "business" and "ethics" in the same sentence without succumbing to the wry humor that certain contradictions attract. The tension between the terms hints at larger concerns implicit in any discussion of business ethics. The point is whether the field is able to pose fundamental questions about capitalism itself as a mode of organizing economic life. Business ethics is not oriented toward a discussion of alternatives to capital. In practice, the concerns within the field tend toward ways to ameliorate the deformations of capitalism. In Christian business ethics, the tacit assumption is that it is possible to wed capitalist business practices with the latest interpretations of principles such as love or justice. Given the successful efforts at deregulation and privatization that date back to the Reagan administration, business ethics is an incomplete and inadequate resource to meet the challenges facing the working class in these times. It is akin to a flood plain that tries to mitigate and channel the rising waters of capitalist triumph in every aspect of contemporary life. But that flood plain threatens to drown the working class.

How might the working class gain resources that would address their particular concerns instead of the businesses that employ them? To do so assumes that it is possible to separate workers from their employers, and this separation is absolutely necessary. The prevailing model in the United States is to push employees to identify their interests with their employers'. Covenantal ethicists who want to see the corporation as a "worldly ecclesia" misapprehend the arena in which it is beneficial to seek a healthy sense of community and solidarity. Corporations do encourage solidarity — but it is solidarity with the company rather than with other employees. This model must be replaced with an ethic that enables workers to see common, overlapping interests across company lines. As a small step in this direction, one possibility is to see what new insights are imaginable if the word "business" is replaced by "labor" to form the term "labor ethic." Since a labor ethic, by definition, places the focus on laborers and workers, conversations about priorities for new models of economic organization could be initiated to achieve a participatory economy. A socialism of worker-owned and managed cooperatives that "intercooperate" with each other is one of many possibilities.[6]

Placing the word "protesting" in front of "labor ethic" suggests other considerations. Workers might view energetic opposition to oppressive work conditions as an expression of their personal and collective work ethic just as the iron rollers did at the Columbus Iron Works in Ohio in the 1870s (chapter 4). In sum, this chapter proposes a work ethic that is not about work but about workers — a labor ethic that is about possibilities for resistance, not rationales for acquiescence. A "protesting" labor ethic is a means by which solutions to the plight of workers can arise. It is meant to be an intervention against any version of Protestantism or its ethic that legitimizes demands made upon workers that diminish their personhood or self-determination. This labor ethic is unapologetic about promoting the material interests of workers. It does not strive for ethical neutrality or moral objectivity. It highlights and even promotes, when necessary, the positive dimensions of conflict for advancing the good of laborers by a transformation of structural inequities in the workplace.

The points of orientation for a protesting labor ethic consist of imagination, a long memory, and a commitment to struggle. Each point is a moment in this ethic, and no one moment has priority over the others. Each part of the ethic informs and is guided by the others. Imaginative activities of resistance that give rise to even more inventive ways of responding to the repression of workers is essential. This aspect of a protesting labor ethic, imagination, has a forward-looking orientation. But to insure that it remains relevant and a lively inspiration, it must be grounded in current struggles — the history that is made daily.[7] Short-term memories of gains and losses eventually become the long memory of the multiple histories of the working class. These histories must be courageous enough to recall not only the victories but also the defeats, and even those losses that dominant members of the working class inflict

---

6. See Bob Stone, "Intercooperation and the Co-op Movement: A Proposal," *GEO Newsletter* (April/May 1997): 1–2. Also Michael W. Howard, *Self-Management and the Crisis of Socialism: The Rose in the Fist of the Present* (Lanham, Md.: Rowman & Littlefield, 2000); Len Krimerman and Frank Lindenfeld, eds., *When Workers Decide: Workplace Democracy Takes Root in North America* (Philadelphia: New Society Publishers, 1992), and bimonthly issues of *GEO Newsletter: Grassroots Economic Organizing, The Newsletter for Democratic Workplaces and Globalization from Below* (www.geonewsletter.org and www.geo.coop).

7. Daniel Singer, *Whose Millennium? Theirs or Ours?* (New York: Monthly Review Press, 1999), 260.

on others. Racism and white supremacy, which make true solidarity in the working class impossible, is an ongoing example. Finally, the commitment to struggle strives to close the gap between what is and what needs to be. The various struggles of a protesting labor ethic could make the leaps of imagination successful ones. The struggles must be worker-based and worker-determined. Any ethic that proscribes, at the outset, forms of struggle and forms of worker activity has to be resisted in favor of worker self-determination.

Imagination and a "Protesting" Labor Ethic

One spark that has inspired imaginations worldwide was set on January 1, 1994, when the Zapatista National Liberation Army from Chiapas celebrated the inauguration of NAFTA with the occupation of the city hall at San Cristóbal de las Casas in Mexico. Almost six years later, the shock waves that had been bouncing around the world had one remarkable reverberation when protesters in Seattle nearly shut down the meeting of the World Trade Organization in November 1999.[8] Since that historic protest, in city after city, from Washington, D.C., to Prague, Quebec City, and Genoa, people have risen up, raised voices, and turned worldwide attention to the once opaque acronyms of international financial institutions and trade agreements. Not all members of the Christian ethics guild have been appreciative of these efforts. Max Stackhouse, in the introduction to the second volume of the *God and Globalization* series, has assured us that the meeting of the World Trade Organization in Seattle was a failure — for the official delegates and also for the protesters. The possibility that the meeting failed because the protests were so successful is not broached. He quotes with approval C. Fred Alford's idea that the participants in both the WTO meetings and the street protest were "merely confused." Furthermore, Stackhouse opined that the "opposition coalition neither stopped globalization nor altered its course."[9] Stackhouse shows his own befuddlement in the face of rein-

---

8. For more about the events in Seattle, see Eddie Yuen, George Katsiaficas, Daniel Burton Rose, eds., *The Battle of Seattle: The New Challenges to Capitalist Globalization* (New York: Soft Skull Press, 2001).

9. Max L. Stackhouse, "Introduction," *The Spirit and the Modern Authorities*, vol. 2 of *God and Globalization: Theological Ethics and the Spheres of Life*, ed. Max L. Stackhouse with Don S. Browning (Harrisburg, Pa.: Trinity Press International, 2001), 4.

vigorated protesters around the world who have put the proponents of untrammeled capitalist economic globalization on the defensive.[10]

The World Social Forums in Brazil have served as initial steps to answer critics of the anti-corporate globalization movement who argue that the protesters in particular and the movement in general have been unable to formulate positive economic alternatives. Local leftists and city administrations contributed $1.5 million for the second annual event in 2002, hosted by the city of Porto Alegre. The meeting attracted fifty thousand delegates from around the world (more than triple the number of a year before). With hundreds of speakers and panels, the Forums have featured a panoply of activists, intellectuals, and organizations for progressive social change who have tried to imagine alternatives to capitalist globalization. From women's advocacy groups to worker cooperatives, the emphasis has not been on forging one theme, a single manifesto or plan of action as a top-down blueprint for an anti-capitalist agenda. Rather, the mere fact of these gatherings and the increasing attention they have gained from first-world elites suggests that imaginative new alternatives to neoliberalism are in the first stages of development. As one speaker at the first convening of the World Social Forum said, "We are here to show the world that another world is possible." The cheering that followed, according to a leading activist and intellectual of the globalization protests, was not for a "specific other world, just the possibility of one."[11] "Another World Is Possible" became the theme for the second social forum in 2002.

The municipal government of Porto Alegre has set an important example for the delegates. The mayor is a member of the Workers Party (Partido dos Trabalhadores, the PT), and the city has been under the party's governance since the late 1980s. The city is guided by a model of citizen involvement at the local level that includes participatory budget planning by local neighborhood and community "issue councils." The residents vote directly to decide on budget priorities ranging from road construction to health care centers. Public service budgets for the poor have increased and citizen participation in government continues

---

10. See Joseph E. Stiglitz, *Globalization and Its Discontents* (New York: W. W. Norton, 2002).

11. Naomi Klein, "Farewell to 'The End of History': Organization and Vision in Anti-Corporate Movements," in *A World of Contradictions: Socialist Register 2002*, ed. Leo Panitch and Colin Leys (London: Merlin Press, 2001), 1.

to grow.[12] Despite the progressive local work, multinational corporations are still a factor. But as one North American delegate to the World Social Forum reported, a motto in Porto Alegre is "Resist and Build," which suggests that the activist citizen base there holds construction and development projects to some standard of accountability.

From the perspective of a protesting labor ethic, the Workers Party in Brazil stands in defiant opposition to those critics of the left who claim there is simply no alternative. It holds power in two hundred municipalities in Brazil. It has mounted a number of very credible campaigns for the Brazilian presidency with Luís Ignácio da Silva, popularly known as "Lula," as its candidate. He is a leader of CUT (Central Unica dos Trabalhadores) in Brazil and a former metal worker.[13] The Workers Party has deep roots in the Brazilian trade union movement. The ability of workers in Brazil to forge a new politics that addresses their issues as laborers is a significant development that reflects great imagination and determination. While the Workers Party is certainly not above criticism, there is promise in this party that is oriented around the interests of the working class.

Long Memories and a "Protesting" Labor Ethic

A study of labor history must be part of any attempt to construct an ethic that advocates a particular stance of labor toward capital. Otherwise, when one invokes ethical norms to address a current labor issue or controversy, one does so in a historical vacuum. Then there is no way to see how such norms have been exemplified in concrete circumstances. Norms become abstract, distant from lived experience, and thus unreliable as a guide because they are untested by the possible limits that their practice might impose on them. The sketch in chapter 5 of company unions and the federal legislation designed to meet those corporate challenges is one example. Most contemporary covenantal Christian ethicists in their advocacy of the norm of cooperation show little or no awareness of the history of labor. The struggle that led to the federal legislation that curbed the corporate muzzle on independent labor voices is all but forgotten. A firmer grasp of this history, possibly, would temper the more

---

12. Naomi Klein, "Coming Together at the Seams," *In These Times*, March 18, 2002, 16.

13. Kim Moody, *Workers in a Lean World: Unions in the International Economy* (London and New York: Verso, 1997), 208–9.

exuberant praises for covenantal relations between labor and management on the basis of not only an empirical but also a legal perspective.
The situation at the Saturn Corporation described in chapter 2 is another example of how the norm of cooperation is found wanting once
the results of its practice become evident.

There are other reasons why a study of labor history must be part
of a protesting labor ethic. The ethos of a labor ethic must be shaped
by the voices, the stories and traditions, and the songs of laborers who
supply content and substance to the term "labor." Such resources help to
ensure that the labor ethic does not eventually become yet another tool
for continued mastery over workers. If a labor ethic is nurtured within
its own history and context, then it is able to speak authentically to
workers because it is their own story. Only then can it become a mode
for empowerment and emancipation for workers to speak forcefully and
authoritatively to their opponents. Workers who engage in this oppositional work become activist-intellectuals who are the best champions and
guardians of their interests. For workers who are activist-intellectuals,
labor history is not so much the source of their action but a necessary
moment of their actions.[14] In the course of their actions, such workers
simultaneously draw upon labor history as one source for their oppositional work and by so doing contribute to it. That is, labor history does
not, in some idealist sense, have such power by itself. It is the engagement of workers with their own stories who stoke the possibility of even
more effective struggle in the future. In this way, workers learn more
about where they have come from and are reinvigorated in the quest for
where they wish to be.

The world of the worker is made up of many facets. It can include the
history of one's working-class family or the broader working-class community in which one labors.[15] The history of a particular work process
itself or the social struggles that shape the content of one's work could
be subjects for a labor history. The working conditions or the shape of
the social relations between workers are other subjects. A chronicle of
strikes or oppositional activity by workers could be the focus.[16]

---

14. Jean-Paul Sartre, *Search for a Method*, trans. Hazel E. Barnes (New York: Vintage Books, 1968), 32.

15. Michael Keith Honey, ed., *Black Workers Remember: An Oral History of Segregation, Unionism, and the Freedom Struggle* (Berkeley: University of California Press, 1999).

16. Jeremy Brecher, *Strike!* rev. ed. (Boston: South End Press, 1997).

The "history" of labor history itself is an important activity because it can show the deformations within the traditioning process. Which histories count and which do not? Or better yet, which workers count and which ones are forgotten? Labor historian David Brody points to Herbert Gutman's essay "Work, Culture, and Society in Industrializing America, 1815–1919."[17] Brody calls it a "pioneering" essay because it breaks out of the "confining limits of trade-union history."[18] Practitioners of this type of study are, for Brody, the "new" labor historians. "Old labor" historians are those trained in the Wisconsin school of John R. Commons, who place the focus on the institutional expressions of labor and not on the workers themselves.[19] The focus on workers is the point of the new labor history. For a protesting labor ethic, it is necessary that this new history be constantly under revision as it deals with the incomplete accounts of the history of labor in the United States. A recent example of this type of history is Venus Green's *Race on the Line: Gender, Labor, and Technology in the Bell System, 1880–1980.* Green demonstrates how race, class, and gender come together to form a compelling account of the experiences of Bell operators, women of color, and their difficult relations with white male bosses.[20]

The almost total invisibility of lesbian, gay, bisexual, and transgendered workers in the workplace, organized and unorganized, is slowly changing due to actions of workers at work and the accounts that chronicle protest and agitation.[21] Without these accounts, "solidarity" becomes an empty word for a labor history unworthy of the name because of its exclusivity. Historical work must be inclusive in character.[22]

---

17. Herbert G. Gutman, "Work, Culture, and Society in Industrializing America, 1815–1919," in *Work, Culture, and Society in Industrializing America: Essays in American Working-Class and Social History* (New York: Vintage Books, 1977), 3–78.

18. David Brody, "The Old Labor History and the New: In Search of the American Working Class," *The Labor History Reader,* ed. Daniel J. Leab (Urbana: University of Illinois Press, 1985), 1–27.

19. Philip S. Foner's ten-volume *History of the Labor Movement in the United States* (New York, International Publishers) is another example of "old" labor history although Foner's attention to gender and race distinguishes his work from his contemporaries.

20. Venus Green, *Race on the Line: Gender, Labor, and Technology in the Bell System, 1880–1980* (Durham, N.C.: Duke University Press, 2001). Another recent treatment of gender, class, and labor history issues can be found in Johanna Brenner, *Women and the Politics of Class* (New York: Monthly Review Press, 2000).

21. Kitty Krupat and Patrick McCreery, *Out at Work: Building a Gay-Labor Alliance* (Minneapolis: University of Minnesota Press, 2001). Also see the journal *New Labor Forum* 8 (spring/summer 2001). The theme of this issue is "Labor Comes Out."

22. For recent work in women's labor history, see Ava Baron, ed., *Work Engendered: Toward a New History of American Labor* (Ithaca, N.Y.: Cornell University Press, 1991). Other

A labor history that romanticizes the working class turns labor history into a hall of heroes. This is a mistake. For example, the labor struggles of 1877 chronicled in chapter 4 are deeply problematic for a number of reasons. The ferocity of the anti-Chinese rioting and violence perpetrated by workers in San Francisco should leave no doubt that labor history should also be a chronicle of the divisions within the working class.[23] Standard accounts of this year might also lead one to believe that white workers were open to and embraced solidarity with black workers all the way from Galveston to Martinsburg. In St. Louis, while white workers yelled out "We will!" to black worker demands for solidarity, words were not followed by actions. Despite the participation of blacks in the Executive Committee that conducted the strike and the delegations that negotiated with the mayor of St. Louis, press reports also showed that white strike leaders wanted to avoid the participation of black workers. Even more ominously, the strike committee wanted to deputize five hundred "special policemen" who would "clean out" black workers from those involved in the strike activity. Later recollections on the part of an Executive Committee leader, Albert Currlin, said that the wish to avoid too close identification with black workers curtailed public mobilizations of workers.[24] This is a tantalizing suggestion. Accounts of the direction and eventual collapse of the strike fail to examine systematically racial animosity as a factor in the eventual decline of working-class rule in St. Louis. Rather, the accounts of the isolated instances of some degree of racial harmony and solidarity during the Great Strikes of 1877 seem to trump the necessary closer examination of the endemic racism that may well have doomed the prospects for even greater worker victories in St. Louis and possibly around the country.

The experience in St. Louis is but one moment in the long history of divisions in the working class and the ways that historical accounts fail to account fully for this phenomenon. The simultaneous necessity for and regret over the unfulfilled promises of working-class history as an element for a protesting labor ethic points to related difficulties in a covenantal ethic and the appropriate responses to such an ethic. The

---

sources include Rosalyn Baxandall and Linda Gordon, eds., *America's Working Women: A Documentary History, 1600 to the Present*, rev. ed. (New York: W. W. Norton, 1995) and *Alice Kessler-Harris, Out to Work: A History of Wage-Earning Women in the United States* (Oxford and New York: Oxford University Press, 1982).

23. Robert V. Bruce, *1877: Year of Violence* (Indianapolis: Bobbs-Merrill, 1959), 266–70.

24. David R. Roediger, *The Wages of Whiteness: Race and the Making of the American Working Class*, rev. ed. (London and New York: Verso, 1999), 167–68.

dismaying inattention to the disparities of power between covenanting parties has been an important factor in the analysis and critique thus far of the covenantal business ethic. Still more disquieting in this ethic is the level of abstraction about the parties who are enjoined to engage in covenanting activity. Differences in race, ethnicity, gender, and sexual orientation are not discussed or considered relevant considerations in the construction of a covenantal business ethic. The supposition is that covenant, as a God-given structuring principle in the lives of created beings, naturally covers everyone. The goal, then, is to recognize one's place in the covenantal order. The possibility that covenants are only historical constructs subject to the limitations of those whose interests are supported and legitimated by such constructs is never discussed or scrutinized.

Appeals to the close relationship between covenant, community, and the common good aim to reinforce the idea that covenantal activity is one of inclusion. However, the sentiment that "the pursuit of the common good would affirm a shared good, a community in common, that is more than the sum of its individual parts and private interests"[25] is the surest way to forget the diverse people who *are* the individual parts. It neglects the ways that distinctive contributions emerge and particular struggles are waged and endured. One cannot assume that the constitutive elements that structure a person's or group's experience of the "good" is experienced in the same way for everyone.

A protesting labor ethic must examine its own premises. Even as it tries to redress the imbalance of power between labor and capital, it cannot simply replicate the covenantalist indifference to the complexity of human experience. The appeal to class alone is very tempting because of the extraordinary historical precedent that views class as the principal formative aspect of human experience. But despite its greatly supposed unifying power, class never has and never will transcend the differences of race, ethnicity, gender, and sexual orientation. This point is not a source of regret but the necessary opening, and liberation, for further exploration. The attention to history in all its forms must be a feature of a protesting labor ethic to help it avoid the pitfalls that it decries in others. A protesting labor ethic must always be a work in process.

---

25. Eric Mount Jr., *Covenant, Community, and the Common Good: An Interpretation of Christian Ethics* (Cleveland: Pilgrim Press, 1999), 97.

"Protest" as well becomes an empty word if it is abstracted from the lived experiences of workers who face the depredations of management *and* of their fellow workers. Historical work in labor studies must always take such matters into account. In this way, labor history can be a source of inspiration for those who try to understand their current work life through the lens of what once was. For those who try to build a new world from the ashes of the old, possibilities of how to avoid the foibles of the old world may become more apparent. Finally, the possibility that one might take some pride in one's status as a member of the working class is enhanced to the degree that one can identify or, at least, recognize the tradition from which one comes. The wish to gloss over and conveniently forget where one has come from is easier if one's working-class tradition is poorly understood or even maligned. A study of the history of labor might make it possible for workers newly arrived in the middle and professional classes to identify with their past rather than with elite interests. Most members of the middle and professional classes would rather forget that they have much more in common, economically, with their brothers and sisters in the factories and service industries across the United States than they ever will with the true economic elites.

Commitment to Struggle: Priority of Labor over Capital

The priority of labor over capital echoes a cardinal doctrine of liberation theology, namely, the preferential option for the poor. Of course, most of the working class in the United States are in vastly different circumstances than those in the two-thirds world who are either dispossessed, refugees, or permanently jobless. Yet the working class in the United States is still highly susceptible to financial disaster in the face of any economic downturns. Most have no appreciable savings, and the equity in a home, if one even has a home, is not a viable means to sustain a suddenly unemployed worker for any length of time. Outside of the top 20 percent of the U.S. population in terms of wealth, only the following quintile or second highest 20 percent can sustain current consumption patterns without a job for more than three months. The rest of the population has either a month before reserves run out or no time at all.[26]

---

26. Chuck Collins, Betsy Leondar-Wright, Holly Sklar, eds., *Shifting Fortunes: The Perils of the Growing American Wealth Gap* (Boston: United for a Fair Economy, 1999), 24.

Elaborate justifications for the priority of labor over capital could be proffered here. When every measure of wealth distribution in this country shows a vast and growing disproportion of liquid and fixed assets in favor of the top 1 percent of the population in the United States, toppling this disproportion in favor of those who have been at the losing ends of the income and wealth scale assumes priority. According legitimacy to labor's attempts to reverse, or at least mitigate, such disparities must be the basic project of a protesting labor ethic.

The priority of labor requires that the voices of workers be respected. The attention to unionized autoworkers in chapter 2 and nonunionized aluminum can producers in the last chapter shows the range of places and conditions under which participation programs thrive. Yet what does one do if statistics show that laborers want to be involved in participation programs? After all, it is not as if these programs are universally unpopular with workers. In unionized workplaces that are distressingly indifferent to sexual harassment, race and gender discrimination, and heterosexism, employee participation programs do appeal to workers who are confident that such issues will be resolved, or even preempted altogether, by employee-management teams. Workers are rightfully upset with the mismanagement of their union locals, the lack of internal union democracy, the exorbitant salaries of union officials, the reluctance to commit resources to organizing new workers, and the "business unionist" orientation that only serves rather than empowers workers.[27]

For workers who are accustomed to being ignored or patronized by their employers, employee participation programs appeal to those who want a more meaningful and interesting workplace. Deborah Wirtz's testimony before the Dunlop Commission on the introduction of employee teams at Texas Instruments represents the views of more than a few workers: "What I really feel, my honest feelings about teaming, is that my self-esteem has improved as a person. Before teaming, you felt like you were maybe a number that was there to produce the daily quota that was expected of you, and you left and went home. Now we feel like we have the capability of making decisions and being heard."[28]

The interest in employee participation programs warrants mention of Richard B. Freeman and Joel Rogers's recent book, *What Workers Want*.

---

27. Two organizations that are dedicated to union democracy are the Association for Union Democracy (*www.uniondemocracy.org*) and Labor Notes (*www.labornotes.org*).

28. Commission on the Future of Worker-Management Relations, *Fact Finding Report* (Washington, D.C.: GPO, 1994), 31.

In this comprehensive survey, which has received widespread attention from both the labor movement and the business lobby, the authors conclude that when "given a choice, workers want 'more' — more say in the workplace decisions that affect their lives, more employee involvement at their firms, more legal protection at the workplace, and more union representation."[29] What does "more" actually mean? Freeman and Rogers used a "split question" design to ferret out the complexities. One half of their sample was asked whether they preferred unions and the other half was asked about "employee organizations that negotiate" (a phrase used to indicate a union but to factor out bias against the term "union"). Twenty-three percent of the former sample responded favorably and 31 percent of the latter. Given that less than 14 percent of all employees actually belong to unions, the opportunities for union organizing are enormous.

As for employee involvement and participation programs, the Freeman and Rogers survey shows that for those who were given the option of unions, 61 percent preferred joint employee-management committees; for the other half of the sample, 55 percent preferred such committees. This undifferentiated statistic has been heralded as the final overwhelming proof that employee participation programs are, indeed, what workers want. The pro-business Labor Policy Institute, in an article for its website, "TEAM Act Would Deregulate Workplace Cooperation," refers to the Freeman and Rogers study and claims that 63 percent of the sampled workers chose such committees.[30] Not emphasized by the LPA and other partisans of employee involvement programs is one essential detail: there are three separate subsections that compose the total percentage of the respondents who prefer joint committees. The preferences include "strongly independent" committees, "somewhat independent" committees, and, third, committees that have no independence (and those who prefer no organization at all). For the survey that included the word "union," 22 percent wanted joint committees that are "strongly independent." For the sample that used the phrase "employee organizations that negotiate," 20 percent chose "strongly independent" committees of employees and management. If one combines the percentage of workers who want unions (or employee organizations that negotiate) with the

---

29. Richard B. Freeman and Joel Rogers, *What Workers Want* (Ithaca, N.Y.: ILR Press, 1999), 154.
30. "TEAM Act Would Deregulate Workplace Cooperation," *www.lpa.org.*

respondents who want strongly independent joint committees of workers and management, one could also conclude that the largest response
for both surveys places emphasis on a deeply independent voice in the
workplace.[31]

A labor ethic needs to accord priority to the voices and desires of
workers. If workers are in favor of participation or employee involvement
programs, this wish ought to be taken seriously and honored. The nu-
merical results of Freeman and Rogers's work are not unambiguous and
admit to varied interpretations. But it is abundantly clear that, overall, workers want more of a say. Yet workers do not want a false say,
they do not wish to be patronized and they do not want to be told they
have power, when, in fact, they do not. This is an issue that is often
overlooked in assessments of who is for and against such participation
programs.

Social Movement Unionism

The focus on unionized workers in this book is not meant to disparage
the concerns of unorganized laborers. Whether part of organized labor or
not, every worker is part of a larger community of workers with certain
shared interests and goals. The hope is that such shared interests and
goals can result in an organized method of resistance and struggle to
attain them. As such, a protesting labor ethic must repeatedly advocate
the legitimacy and useful function of the modern labor union. Such a
stance is hardly militant by historical standards. After all, an advocacy of
unionization can be merely a new call for the same old business unionism
discussed in the last chapter. Instead, labor unions must cultivate their
social-political role as a force for advocacy, activism, and agitation. In
this view, immediate ends such as the next contract, a better pension,
and a higher salary would be regarded as excellent first steps but not
the final point of the journey. This necessary and more comprehensive
outlook for workers is that of international social-movement unionism.
Kim Moody outlines the main points of this unionism in his *Workers in
a Lean World*.

According to Moody, a social-movement unionism comprises an entire orientation for workers who need to be in the forefront of all struggles
that affect their own lives. Such unionism does not simply "support" a

---

31. Freeman and Rogers, *What Workers Want*, 151.

political party or candidate favorable to its aims and hope they will do the right thing once in power. Rather, it is a powerful force itself as its unionized workers reach out to other social movements. "Social-movement unionism implies an active strategic orientation that uses the strongest of society's oppressed and exploited, generally organized workers, to mobilize those who are less able to sustain self-mobilization: the poor, the unemployed, the casualized workers, the neighborhood organizations."[32] This can occur only if the unions themselves are democratic. An energetic rank and file outside the union hall is the outcome of engaged workers struggling to maintain democracy within their union.

Strategies of social-movement unionism include the development of bargaining positions that help not only the union but also those outside the union and in the surrounding community. Moody calls this a harmonization of collective bargaining and class interests. For instance, a union would agitate for the preservation, or even increase, of employment in related industries as part of its own set of demands. Other examples include unions that bargain for restrictions in outsourcing. Or if outsourcing is agreed upon, then it is stipulated that the work goes to unionized shops. The Saturn Corporation and the initial agreement forged with the UAW for employment at the Spring Hill, Tennessee, plant is an interesting example of the failure to consider a social-movement union approach. There was no attempt to enfranchise the surrounding area at the outset; instead the initial hires were transplants from already existing or recently closed down GM plants from around the country.

In sum, social-movement unionism calls for the reformation of existing unions so that they are democratic and have a leadership that is accountable to its members. The members of the union must be involved to increase the scope of its organizing. Not only must the union expand in numbers but other parts of the working class must be engaged in the common struggle against the predations of international capitalism.[33]

Workers' Centers

Social-movement unionism is a promising alternative to unions that merely provide services to the membership or unions that, in cooper-

---

32. Moody, *Workers in a Lean World*, 276. "Casualized" workers are those with part-time, temporary, or occasional work status.

33. This summary of social-movement unionism is indebted to Kim Moody's more extensive formulation in the conclusion and epilogue of *Workers in a Lean World*, 269–310.

ation with management, deliver a contract every two or three years
but are otherwise disengaged from the membership. The possibilities for
social-movement unionism are enormous and the task of democratizing
unions to enable this to occur must go on. As noted above, this unionism uses the "strongest of society's oppressed and exploited," usually
organized workers, to mobilize those who are less able to sustain self-
mobilization. Thus one must pause to consider another extraordinary
sector of the labor movement, which is neither organized nor considered
strong because of its place in the labor hierarchy: sweatshop workers.

A persuasive account of sustained worker resistance is aptly summed
up in the title of a book on immigrant women workers, *Sweatshop Warriors*. Author Miriam Ching Yoon Louie, through firsthand accounts and
interviews with sweatshop workers, shows how through the "very act of
speaking their minds," women workers have "challenged multiple layers
of oppression" and have undergone the transition from workers to warriors.[34] The context for this transition has been the immigrant workers'
centers. "The ethnic-based workers' centers reach, organize, and defend
the immigrant, low-waged, ethnic minority women workers who are not
protected by the trade union movement."[35] Housed in storefronts and
community centers, the "workers' centers are a bit like small guerrilla
warriors fighting a more heavily armed opponent."[36]

> The centers offer workers an infrastructure that enables them to
> take advantage of the experiences and expertise accumulated in
> prior struggles, develop their consciousness and leadership, con-
> nect with other workers and organizations, act as part of a broader
> movement, and begin to alter the power relations within the
> industries and communities where they work and live.[37]

Similar to social-movement unionism, they have the broader aspiration
of reaching out to other workers to build the larger organizational force
necessary to topple oppressive power structures. They are the type of
organization that a social-movement unionism would seek to reach. But
the workers' centers, according to Louie, have to weigh the effects of

---

34. Miriam Ching Yoon Louie, *Sweatshop Warriors: Immigrant Women Workers Take on
the Global Factory* (Cambridge, Mass.: South End Press, 2001), 13.
35. Ibid., 216.
36. Ibid., 218.
37. Ibid., 218–19.

cooperating with unions, such as UNITE (Union of Needle Trades, Industrial and Textile Employees) who have protected their relationships with employers and manufacturers to the detriment of the workers.[38] The immigrant workers' centers struggle against the gender-specific character or the resegregation of sweatshops. Women unite across language, ethnic, and cultural barriers to make the issue of sweatshops visible, gain whatever measure of justice is possible from their employers, and, all the while, call attention to the opportunities for further organizing and educational efforts.

Tactics for Troublemaking

A protesting labor ethic considers conflict a vital matter in any discussion about the workplace. The already existing conflictual relations between labor and capital is one aspect. The advocacy of conflict when such means will achieve the interests of laborers is also part of this ethic. Coercion, violence, and sabotage cannot be ruled out to achieve material parity or even ascendancy over corporate interests. Though not removed from consideration, conflict is not an ethical ideal and sought out for its own sake. Conflict is only one resource for ameliorating the social ills that gave rise to it. Guided by history and attentive to both the pitfalls and promises of direct action against oppression, this ethic is historical and material at its base. It emphasizes flexibility in relationship to the workers' best reading of a given situation or historical moment.

Direct action cannot be taken on behalf of the workers. If workers decide to initiate such activities, then they are the legitimate authorities to execute the plan of resistance. Workers may seek out allies or may accept the initiation of relationships from community groups, activists, students, and maybe even academics.[39] But, in the end, workers must live with the consequences of their actions. At best, they will achieve their aims. At worst, they will be the ones to suffer the backlash from their employers and the repressive state apparatus. The source of the workers' authority is their own lives and their own future. Some say that

---

38. Ibid., 244, n. 15.

39. Steven Fraser and Joshua B. Freeman, *Audacious Democracy: Labor, Intellectuals, and the Social Reconstruction of America* (Boston: Houghton Mifflin, 1997). See Albert Nolan's comments on academics and workers in his essay "A Worker's Theology" in *The Three-Fold Cord: Theology, Work and Labour,* ed. James R. Cochrane and Gerald O. West (Hilton, South Africa: Cluster Publications, 1991), 160–68.

the advocacy of direct action constitutes "class war," but "class war" is already a fair description of capitalist activity in the United States and around the world.

The assumption that gives rise to the possibility of conflict as an aspect of working-class resistance is that the capitalist class will not willingly and peacefully hand over benefits, compensation, or control in the workplace. If this assumption is true, then what recourse is available? The way that one answers this question places one in the continuum ranging from worker acquiescence to forming unions to armed struggle. Rather than aiming at a specific point or range on this continuum, another approach is to think ahead about the intentions of capital for the conditions of production and the workplace. In this way, one can think about appropriate responses.

The experience of workers at the Saturn Corporation is exactly the right place to consider the intentions of capital in the next decades. Of the five Saturn values that every worker must embody, teamwork and continuous improvement are borrowed directly from the new work paradigm that is at the heart of the new economy — lean production. Lean production tries to do away with the "buffers" of traditional mass production. In the auto industry these have included "high inventories, large stockpiles between work stations, excessive space, including large repair areas, and a corps of relief workers to cover for absentees."[40] Instead, lean production emphasizes "just-in-time" delivery (rather than stocking inventory in-house), standardized work, and continuous cost reduction.

Saturn learned a great deal from another important example of labor-management cooperation — the CAMI plant located in Ontario. CAMI is a joint venture of General Motors and Suzuki announced in 1986. It was intended to be a showcase of the virtues and benefits of lean production. Like Saturn, CAMI has company values that guide work activity. These include empowerment, *kaizen*, open communication, and team spirit. *Kaizen*, or continuous incremental improvement, is realized through the team concept. Saturn followed the CAMI example of regarding the whole company as one team: "Everyone employed by CAMI, from the top to the bottom of the organization, is regarded as a member

---

40. James Rinehart, Christopher Huxley, and David Robertson, *Just Another Car Factory? Lean Production and Its Discontents* (Ithaca, N.Y.: ILR Press, 1997), 25.

of one big company team that pulls together to attain company goals."[41] A major responsibility of the team is to submit suggestions for quality improvement. A suggestion, or a *teian*, is at the heart of *kaizen*, or continuous improvement. Workers are strongly encouraged to develop and turn in *teians* to the company.

The design for the Saturn Corporation also drew upon the latest research in the field. Perhaps most influential of all was the national best-seller, *The Machine That Changed the World: The Story of Lean Production*. Published in 1990 it was a crushing indictment of traditional mass production and an unapologetic cheerleader for lean production. Among other promised benefits, it assured readers that only half the amount of human effort in the factory would be required relative to mass production.[42] Another resource for Saturn planners has been Peter Senge's *The Fifth Discipline: The Art and Practice of the Learning Organization*.[43] This book is designed to help companies become learning organizations and to ensure that worker teams develop ways to continually assure the free exchange of information. Both books have been heralded as answers to the old world of top-down authoritarian workplaces. Neither book has anything to say about the effects of lean production on workers or about what is owed to laborers who are doing all the learning but gain little in compensation or control over the workplace.

The complaints of Saturn workers about continuous improvement, overwork, and injuries are symptomatic of the problems with this new work paradigm. The principles of lean production, aided and abetted by continual advances in information technology, are making their way into every nook and cranny of the workplace. Sweatshops, where production seems leanest of all with not even a spare second in a minute, arise as a result of lean production's drive to cut costs and improve efficiency. From data entry workers whose every key stroke is monitored and timed by yet other computers, to poultry workers whose bathroom breaks are timed or simply not allowed, to all the forms of workplace surveillance to monitor and improve efficiency,[44] the workplace is hyper-

41. Ibid., 91.

42. James P. Womack, Daniel T. Jones, and Daniel Roos, *The Machine That Changed the World: The Story of Lean Production* (New York: HarperPerennial, 1991), 13.

43. Peter M. Senge, *The Fifth Discipline: The Art and Practice of the Learning Organization* (New York: Currency Doubleday, 1994); originally published in 1990.

44. Nancy Bupp, "Big Brother and Big Boss Are Watching You," *WorkingUSA: The Journal of Labor and Society* 5, no. 2 (fall 2001): 69–81.

Taylorized, underregulated, and just plain dangerous. Lean production is even knocking on the door of higher education.[45] In 1999, 1.7 million workplace injuries were reported for all workplaces in the United States. Over a third involved repetitive motion injuries that are typical for workers in auto plants.[46] From 1980 to 1995, more than ninety-three thousand U.S. workers died on the job.[47] Temporary and contingent work is a method to shape the workforce into a flexible instrument that can expand or contract, as a corporation deems fit, to ensure profitability and maximum return for stockholders.

When critics of the anti-capitalist globalization movement argue that all the protesters are simply anti-globalist, they fail to grasp that the main aspect of the protests is to ask, very publicly, the following questions: Who will decide who will benefit from globalization? To whom are the structures of global finance and credit accountable? Who will decide the pace and the eventual extent of the features of a global economy? Kim Moody's discussion of social-movement unionism above is helpful. Social-movement unionism must include the internationalization of union links and coordination with activists who are not in unions. This will open the way to globalize the struggle against the globalization of capitalism and its methods of production — especially lean production.

According to Moody, transnational worker networks are one vehicle for this struggle. Such networks consist of workers in similar industries who gather across borders to promote worker education, conferences, and meetings. This leads to the possibility that coordinated local strikes at pivotal points of production around the globe could, in Moody's terms, "cripple even the largest TNCs [transnational corporations] in their major markets."[48] That is, given the ever tighter coordination of production and the ever present need to reduce slack in the system, the power of workers to threaten the delicately calibrated system is enhanced. Inventories that are cut to the barest minimum become opportunities for troublemaking. In March 1996, a strike by three thousand workers in two plants of Delphi, the brake manufacturing division of General Motors, in Dayton, Ohio, produced impressive results. Only days into

45. David F. Noble, *Digital Diploma Mills: The Automation of Higher Education* (New York: Monthly Review Press, 2001).

46. Mary Johnson, "Disabling a Civil Right," *The Nation*, February 11, 2002, 22.

47. The National Institute for Occupational Safety and Health released these results in October 2001 from their study of fatal injuries at work; see Freda Coodin, " 'Carnival of Carnage' in Industry Is No Less Real Than Terrorism," *Labor Notes* (December 2001): 11.

48. Moody, *Workers in a Lean World*, 282.

this seventeen-day strike, twenty-seven out of GM's twenty-nine manufacturing plants in North America closed down. This idled over two
hundred thousand workers in GM and non-GM plants in the United
States, Canada, and Mexico.[49] This is just one possibility in a world of
work that is ever more tightly integrated. The globalization of capitalism that Karl Marx described so presciently in the *Communist Manifesto*
has come to pass. While the challenges are enormous, the opportunities
are abundant. The tasks of cross-border organizing and expanding the
conditions for the international solidarity of workers are more important
than ever.

•

Tactics that avail themselves of new opportunities in the new economy
of lean production are reminiscent of an earlier era when calls for the
"conscious withdrawal of workers' industrial efficiency" were the order
of the day.[50] Whether it is avoiding efficiency or refusing to work at all,
the panoply of ways to keep work (or nonwork) interesting is only as
limited as one's imagination.[51] Cooperation with capital, whether it is
rationalized in economic terms or justified in covenantal terms, has not
achieved its goals. A protesting labor ethic offers a new alternative for a
new economy. It is not assured of success, but it is assuredly worth a try.

Postscript

Perhaps the age of acquiescence is over. Stirrings can be detected all
over the world. From Chiapas in 1994 to Seattle in 1999, from Prague
to Quebec City to Genoa and many places in between, trade union-
ists and workers have joined with students and activists to state clearly
that they have had enough. Hidden policies and secretive deal-making
have been held up to the light of day. The first worldwide longshore
workers' action in history occurred in 1997 when workers in over one
hundred ports showed solidarity with the workers in Liverpool, England,

---

49. Kim Moody, "G.M. Goes Down, Sub-Contracting Goes On," *Labor Notes*, May
1996, 1, 14.

50. Elizabeth Gurley Flynn, "Sabotage: The Conscious Withdrawal of Workers' Industrial Efficiency" (New York: I.W.W., reprinted 2001). Originally published in October 1916
by the I.W.W. Publishing Bureau, Cleveland, Ohio.

51. Or one may turn to Dan La Botz's, *A Troublemaker's Handbook: How to Fight Back
Where You Work — and Win!* (Detroit: Labor Notes, 1991).

facing the privatization of the docks there.[52] Workers and peasants in Bolivia stopped plans there to privatize water supplies in 2000.[53] General strikes in Argentina in December 2001 and January 2002 brought down successive presidencies and called into question Argentinian corporate practices and the role of international finance in the Argentinian economy. In the spring of 2002, over two million Italian workers took to the streets in the first daylong general strike in Italy in many years. More than 13 million workers stayed home in a bid to halt the liberalization of labor laws and to protest the government's suggestion of a link between labor and terrorism. Another world is made possible by the collective action of unified and passionate workers. May the protests continue worldwide.

---

52. Ibid., 9.
53. Vandana Shiva, *Water Wars: Privatization, Pollution, and Profit* (Cambridge, Mass.: South End Press, 2002).

SELECT BIBLIOGRAPHY

Allen, Joseph L. *Love and Conflict: A Covenantal Model of Christian Ethics.* Nashville: Abingdon Press, 1984.

Andolsen, Barbara Hilkert. *Good Work at the Video Display Terminal: A Feminist Ethical Analysis of Changes in Clerical Work.* Knoxville: University of Tennessee Press, 1989.

Bloomquist, Karen L. *The Dream Betrayed: Religious Challenge of the Working Class.* Minneapolis: Fortress Press, 1990.

Bluestone, Barry, and Irving Bluestone. *Negotiating the Future: A Labor Perspective on American Business.* New York: Basic Books, 1992.

Brecher, Jeremy. *Strike!* Rev. ed. Boston: South End Press, 1997.

Bruce, Robert V. *1877: Year of Violence.* Indianapolis: Bobbs-Merrill, 1959.

Burbank, David T. *Reign of the Rabble: The St. Louis General Strike of 1877.* New York: Augustus M. Kelley Publishers, 1966.

Cadman, H. W. *The Christian Unity of Capital and Labor.* Philadelphia: American Sunday School Union, 1888.

De Pree, Max. *Leadership Is an Art.* New York: Bantam Doubleday Dell, 1989.

Flynn, Elizabeth Gurley. "Sabotage: The Conscious Withdrawal of Workers' Industrial Efficiency." Reprint edition. New York: I.W.W., 2001.

Gladden, Washington. *Applied Christianity: Moral Aspects of Social Questions.* Boston: Houghton, Mifflin, 1894.

————. *The Labor Question.* Boston: Pilgrim Press, 1911.

————. *Tools and the Man: Property and Industry under the Christian Law.* Boston: Houghton, Mifflin, 1893.

————. *Working People and Their Employers.* Boston: Lockwood, Brooks, and Company, 1876.

Gutman, Herbert G. *Work, Culture, and Society in Industrializing America: Essays in American Working-Class and Social History.* New York: Vintage Books, 1977.

Harrison, Beverly W. *Making the Connections: Essays in Feminist Social Ethics.* Ed. Carol S. Robb. Boston: Beacon Press, 1985.

Herman, Stewart W. *Durable Goods: A Covenantal Ethic for Management and Employees.* Notre Dame, Ind.: University of Notre Dame Press, 1997.

Hogler, Raymond L., and Guillermo J. Grenier. *Employee Participation and Labor Law in the American Workplace.* New York: Quorum Books, 1992.

Hopkins, C. H. *The Rise of the Social Gospel in American Protestantism, 1865–1915.* New Haven: Yale University Press, 1940.

Krimerman, Len, and Frank Lindenfeld, eds. *When Workers Decide: Workplace Democracy Takes Root in North America.* Philadelphia: New Society Publishers, 1992.

Krupat, Kitty, and Patrick McCreery. *Out at Work: Building a Gay-Labor Alliance.* Minneapolis: University of Minnesota Press, 2001.

La Botz, Dan. *A Troublemaker's Handbook: How to Fight Back Where You Work — and Win!* Detroit: Labor Notes, 1991.

Lafargue, Paul. *The Right to Be Lazy.* Chicago: Charles H. Kerr, 1907.

Le Blanc, Paul. *A Short History of the U.S. Working Class: From Colonial Times to the Twenty-first Century.* Amherst, N.Y.: Humanity Books, an imprint of Prometheus Books, 1999.

Louie, Miriam Ching Yoon. *Sweatshop Warriors: Immigrant Women Workers Take on the Global Factory.* Cambridge, Mass.: South End Press, 2001.

Martin, Joan M. *More Than Chains and Toil: A Christian Work Ethic of Enslaved Women.* Louisville: Westminster John Knox Press, 2000.

May, William F. *The Physician's Covenant: Images of the Healer in Medical Ethics.* 2d ed. Louisville: Westminster John Knox Press, 2000.

Mishel, Lawrence, Jared Bernstein, and John Schmitt. *The State of Working America: 2000/2001.* Ithaca, N.Y.: ILR Press, 2001.

Montgomery, David. *Workers' Control in America: Studies in the History of Work, Technology, and Labor Struggles.* Cambridge: Cambridge University Press, 1979.

Moody, Kim. *An Injury to All: The Decline of American Unionism.* London and New York: Verso, 1988.

———. *Workers in a Lean World: Unions in the International Economy.* London and New York: Verso, 1997.

Mount, Eric, Jr. *Covenant, Community, and the Common Good: An Interpretation of Christian Ethics.* Cleveland: Pilgrim Press, 1999.

O'Toole, Jack. *Forming the Future: Lessons from the Saturn Corporation.* Cambridge, Mass.: Blackwell Publishers, 1996.

Panitch, Leo, and Colin Leys, eds. *A World of Contradictions: Socialist Register 2002.* London: Merlin Press, 2001.

Parker, Mike, and Jane Slaughter. *Working Smart: A Union Guide to Participation Programs and Reengineering.* Detroit: Labor Notes, 1994.

Rauschenbusch, Walter. *Christianity and the Social Crisis.* Louisville: Westminster/John Knox Press, 1991; originally published 1907.

————. *Christianizing the Social Order.* New York: Macmillan, 1921; originally published 1912.

Roediger, David R. *The Wages of Whiteness: Race and the Making of the American Working Class.* Rev. ed. London and New York: Verso, 1999.

Rubinstein, Saul A., and Thomas A. Kochan. *Learning from Saturn: Possibilities for Corporate Governance and Employee Relations.* Ithaca, N.Y.: ILR Press, 2001.

Sherman, Joe. *In the Rings of Saturn.* New York: Oxford University Press, 1994.

Stackhouse, Max L. *Covenant and Commitments: Faith, Family, and Economic Life.* Louisville: Westminster John Knox Press, 1997.

Weber, Max. *The Protestant Ethic and the Spirit of Capitalism.* Trans. Talcott Parsons. New York: Charles Scribner's Sons, 1958.

Womack, James P., Daniel T. Jones, and Daniel Roos. *The Machine That Changed the World: The Story of Lean Production.* New York: HarperPerennial, 1991.

Yates, Michael. *Power on the Job: The Legal Rights of Working People.* Boston: South End Press, 1994.

Zinn, Howard, and Dana Frank, and Robin D. G. Kelley. *Three Strikes: Miners, Musicians, Salesgirls, and the Fighting Spirit of Labor's Last Century.* Boston: Beacon Press, 2001.

Zweig, Michael. *The Working Class Majority: America's Best Kept Secret.* Ithaca, N.Y.: ILR Press, 2000.

INDEX